CARDINAL BASIL HUME

With deepest gratitude to the Benedictine Sisters of Mount Angel, Oregon
for instilling in me a love and appreciation for the Holy Rule
and all things Benedictine.

Cardinal Basil Hume

A Pilgrim's Search for God

Gertrude Feick

GRACEWING

First published in England in 2019
by
Gracewing
2 Southern Avenue
Leominster
Herefordshire HR6 0QF
United Kingdom
www.gracewing.co.uk

ISBN 978 085244 940 0

Typeset by Word and Page, Chester, UK

Cover design by Bernardita Peña Hurtado

Front cover image: Basil Hume by Bern Schwartz
© National Portrait Gallery, London

CONTENTS

ACKNOWLEDGEMENTS

With gratitude to Fr Paul Murray OP, for his unwavering support and detailed guidance with my doctoral thesis, and for recommending my work to Gracewing Publishing; to Tom Longford and the staff at Gracewing; to Abbot Timothy Wright OSB (RIP), for inspiring me to write about Basil Hume; to Abbot Cuthbert Madden OSB and the entire Community at Ampleforth Abbey, for their gracious hospitality and permission to access their archives; to Julia Brooke, for her kind assistance and professionalism; to Liam Kelly, for proofreading and encouragement. With special thanks to all those who trusted me with their memories of Basil Hume: Patrick Barry OSB (RIP), Cecilia Beanland OSB (RIP), Matthew Burns OSB, Adrian Convery OSB, Alban Crossley OSB, Francis Dobson OSB (RIP), Philippa Edwards OSB (who also proofread the text for this book), Joanna Jamieson OSB, Bonaventure Knollys OSB (RIP), Edgar Miller OSB, Dominic Milroy OSB (RIP), Cardinal Cormac Murphy-O'Connor (RIP), Bishop Brian Noble, Archbishop Arthur Roche, Mr Gerard Simpson, Cyprian Smith OSB, Archbishop Rembert G. Weakland OSB, Mr Philip Westmacott. For Charles Borromeo Gonzalez OSB and his help at the Mount Angel Abbey Library. In thanksgiving for Abbess Kathy DeVico OCSO and my sisters at Redwoods Abbey, for wholeheartedly supporting the publication of this book.

FOREWORD

My memories of Cardinal Hume are vivid and enduring. I am not alone in this. Cardinal George Basil Hume touched the lives of many, many people in ways that are not forgotten.

I recall his deep compassion and awareness of the needs of others. This depth of soul was expressed in consistent and effective initiatives for the poor and for those in need both at home and abroad. For all his monastic manner he was a man of action.

But this compassion also expressed itself in his manner as a teacher of the Catholic faith. He always strove to uphold the greater good while never underestimating the importance of our best efforts and strivings, with all their shortcomings.

This compassion was rooted in his keen and constant awareness of his own weaknesses and failings. He knew he depended on the mercy of God. He knew he was, in the phrase of Pope Francis, 'caressed by the Father's mercy', and therefore showed that same mercy to others. The words of St Paul were written deep in his heart: 'The human race has nothing to boast about to God' (1 Cor. 1:29).

I recall the last time I heard him speak in public. It was in St Edward's Church, Golders Green, shortly before he died. He spoke of his own journey towards death, the anxiety he felt and his profound sense of going to his Father to whom he would tell his story, without ambiguity, and with confidence in His loving mercy. He told us that the parable of the Prodigal Son was one of his most favourite Scriptural passages. His words were a witness without parallel.

Cardinal Hume had a rare gift of putting into words, for us all, the struggle involved in reaching out to God. He helped us to understand that only occasionally will we catch a glimpse of God's beauty and goodness. For the most part, we are to live in hopeful trust, knowing that God is near, even if we do not easily or readily sense His presence. I thank God every day for the gift He gave to us in this good Cardinal.

I also thank Sister Gertrude for her painstaking work in researching and preparing this book. She opens for us the depth of Cardinal Hume's spiritual journey, in its consistency, its struggles and its fruitfulness. She renders us all a real service, delivered in a most timely way, as we mark the twentieth anniversary of the death of this great man.

+Cardinal Vincent Nichols
January 2019

Introduction

I like the concept of man being in search of God. Slowly, we come to realize that it is only one way of speaking of our response to God's search for us.

Basil Hume, *To Be a Pilgrim: A Spiritual Notebook*

'Who speaks for Christianity in England?'[1] This question, asked by a journalist on the occasion of Cardinal Basil Hume's sixtieth birthday, was answered without hesitation, by the same journalist, with these words: 'It would be difficult to find anyone more acceptable than Cardinal Basil Hume.'[2] Basil Hume was not a theologian, at least not in the strict sense of the word. He was a monk who became an abbot, and then became an archbishop and cardinal. But, though not in any sense a *scientific* theologian, Hume, to all those who knew him, possessed a distinctive theological and spiritual vision. And that vision—Benedictine through and through—helped him to become a superb leader and guide; first of all, for his fellow monks during his thirteen years as Abbot of Ampleforth, and then, for countless numbers of people in England and elsewhere, during his twenty-three years as Cardinal Archbishop.

During his life, Basil Hume delivered numerous speeches, radio and television broadcasts, homilies, conferences, pastoral letters, and addresses, many of which were later compiled and edited to produce books. Some of these books were published while Hume was still alive; all are still available today, and some have been translated into different languages.

Of the various books and articles written *about* Hume, the most recent is a collection of essays, edited by Hume's nephew William Charles: *Basil Hume: Ten Years On.* In the Foreword to this work, Charles remarks first of all, 'This book is not a biography.'[3] And then he goes on to say: 'Nor does this book seek to provide profound scholarly insights into the spirituality of the subject we cover ... One day, I hope, someone might be inspired to produce a work which would aim to shed light on these matters.'[4]

To answer that particular need and to commemorate the twentieth anniversary of Cardinal Hume's death are the primary motives behind this book, originally a doctoral thesis, the first ever undertaken on Basil Hume. As part of my research, I had the privileged opportunity of conducting 19 interviews with people who knew Basil Hume well, among them fellow monks, nuns, relatives, friends, bishops and archbishops. Since I never met Hume in person, these interviews afforded me important insights into the character and life history of Basil, both as monk and cardinal. Almost nothing, I would say, in a work of this kind, is more authoritative than personal witness. That said, however, there are many different ways of coming close to an author. And, in this case, I like to think that the simple fact of belonging to the same Benedictine tradition as Basil Hume has helped me, and in no small measure at times, not only in the work of research, but also in the task of understanding.

A huge help for my work has been the privileged access I was given to the archives at Ampleforth Abbey. There I was able to read the talks and sermons (approximately 120 in number) which Hume delivered over many years, some of them published, some unpublished. In drawing again and again on archival sources and on published works, my aim throughout has been to allow the authentic voice of Basil Hume to sound loud and clear: the voice of Hume the Man (Chapter 1); Hume the Monk (Chapter 2); Hume the Pastor (Chapter 3); and Hume the Preacher (Chapter 4).

Hume's Benedictine spirituality and his personal dedication to prayer gave him the ability to relate to other pilgrims who seek the living and true God. Hume, the monk, pastor, and preacher, still speaks to contemporary Benedictines, the wider Church, and the world. Even though, as Hume stated, 'In our public life we move further and further away from God and the things of God,'[5] he added, 'in the hearts of men and women I believe that the yearning for God is becoming more and more intense.'[6] That yearning was at the core of Basil Hume's search for God—for Hume, the way of a pilgrim: 'Life in our monastic setting is a search for God—with and in Christ—for the Father. It is a pilgrim way.'[7]

NOTES

[1] C. Howse, 'Christopher Howse Profiles Cardinal Hume at 60', *Catholic Herald* (25 February 1983), p. 5.

[2] *Ibid.*

[3] W. Charles, ed., *Basil Hume: Ten Years On* (London: Burns & Oates, 2009), p. ix.

[4] *Ibid.*

[5] B. Hume, *To Be a Pilgrim: A Spiritual Notebook* (repr. London: SPCK Classics, 2009), p. 47.

[6] *Ibid.*

[7] B. Hume, *Searching for God* (New York: Paulist Press, 1978), p. 60.

Chapter 1

Hume the Man

In the whole question of communicating the word of God it is sincerity that matters: not the clever thought, the neat turn of phrase. What matters is genuine sincerity, which can come through the most banal thought and the clumsiest sentence. How often it is true that it is the man to whom one is listening, not the words he is saying. And surely sincerity has to be the quality of a person who is in contact with Christ Our Lord.

Basil Hume, *Searching for God*

GEORGE HALIBURTON HUME was born on 2 March 1923, the third of five children, in Newcastle-upon-Tyne, United Kingdom. Hume's father, William, was English and a highly respected heart specialist. His mother, Mimi, was French and a devout Catholic. George's upbringing was one of the middle class, yet as a boy George was exposed to the poor and their living conditions near St Dominic's Priory, which stood in a poorer section of Newcastle. He received a solid grounding in the faith and a life of prayer at home. The home environment in which the boy was raised provided the foundation for beliefs he expressed as an adult. Speaking about vocations, Hume said: 'A good religious, if I may call on my own experience, receives his or her first novitiate in the family. The first lessons in prayer are not given in the seminary or novitiate; they are given at home.'[1] The duty of transmitting the Catholic faith and a life of prayer fell predominately to George's mother, yet the cultural influences of both his French mother and English father were formative and expanded his view of the world.

In 1933 George was sent to school at Gilling Castle, a prep-school for Ampleforth College, run by the Benedictine monks at Ampleforth Abbey, Yorkshire, England, members of the English Benedictine Congregation. After his years at Gilling Castle, he continued his studies at Ampleforth College. At the College he excelled at sport, especially rugby. He later became captain of the First XV (the first team), a position that 'carries much status as well as creating a natural circle of friends.'[2] As far as academics, Hume's nephew relates: '[George] remembered hearing his mother say to someone else, "If only George knew as much about his studies as he does about football, he would do very well." He said, "I never forgot that. I knew a lot about football then because I was interested and loved it."'[3]

In 1941, at the age of 18, George entered the Monastic Community at Ampleforth, even though as a boy he imagined that his vocation was with the 'energetic, passionately intellectual Dominicans; but his years with the less flamboyant and less individualistic Benedictines had left their mark.'[4] By choosing to enter the monastery and forgoing service in the Army, he made a decision that weighed heavily on him for the rest of his life. On his choice, Hume told John Mortimer: 'It was a terrible choice. The war was on then and I didn't know whether to go into the Army or become a monk. If it happened again, I think I would have gone into the Army.'[5]

Upon entrance into the monastery, George received the name Basil from Abbot Herbert Byrne. In 1944, Hume went to Oxford to read modern history and in 1945 he made his solemn vows. He gained a Licentiate in Sacred Theology at the University of Fribourg. Ordained priest in 1950, Hume then taught religion, French language and literature, and European history at Ampleforth College. He coached the college First XV rugby team and was a much-loved housemaster. In addition, he taught dogmatic theology to the young monks of the Community. The student and confrère Dominic Milroy commented: 'His theology was, strictly speaking, "pre-Vatican": we are talking about the years 1957–1961.

But the content was both perennial (Thomism, the Fathers of the Church) and prophetic, anticipating the great themes of Vatican II.[6] Well versed in and comfortable with the teaching of Thomas Aquinas, Hume had the freedom and ability to 'go off on all sorts of tangents of his own which had leapt out to him from a particular tractate or particular theme of St Thomas.'[7]

Hume was elected Abbot of Ampleforth in 1963. The context in which he was elected assists in better understanding the scope of his responsibilities. He was elected at the age of 40, succeeding Abbot Byrne who had been abbot for twenty-four years. Byrne was the only abbot Hume ever had, and a man he deeply respected. At the time of Hume's election the Community numbered over 150,[8] most of them ordained priests who served some twenty parishes for which Hume was responsible. Ampleforth College had over 600 students. Hume was also responsible for 'the prep school at Gilling Castle, the House of Studies at Oxford (St Benet's Hall) and the recent foundation in St Louis, USA, which was still directly dependent on Ampleforth, and where there were ten Ampleforth monks.'[9]

Elected during the years of the Second Vatican Council, Hume was called to help better articulate the Benedictine spirituality of the Ampleforth Community and make the necessary adaptations so that their spiritual practices were relevant to the current times. He called this endeavour 'a daunting task'.[10] Early in his tenure, Hume addressed the Community:

> The Church is growing to a new maturity in this twentieth century and inevitably this is going to bring—as periods of growth always do—a certain 'malaise', or certain number of growing pains; and it is important that in our thinking about the things of God we should not be dogmatic on the one hand, or on the other hand, we should not close our minds. Again, in this context, how important is the virtue of humility: it stops us from being dogmatic, and it stops us from taking up positions in the contrary sense. And in our practice I have tried to emphasise how important it

is that what we adopt should be done organically, that is, as a way of growth, and slowly, and always, in order not to upset. I have always had this fear in mind, that if we are too quick or too ardent or perhaps a bit irresponsible, then we could very easily destroy the very thing which we were trying to create: namely, a community living in God. And so, perhaps, some of you think that we move too slowly; but I can assure you that it is wise that it should be so.[11]

Hume was called to embrace his role as Christ the Teacher in the monastery. On the teaching role, he said: 'The Rule of St Benedict tells the Abbot that he must be a teacher who is able to put before his monks things old and new',[12] and the reader of his published monastic conferences 'will notice that at Ampleforth the Abbot himself had to grapple with a variety of problems in order to reconcile the old with the new as the latter were presented by theologians and monastic thinkers.'[13] The archivist at Ampleforth summarized well the conciliar climate at the time of Hume's election as well as the challenges he faced:

> At the election of Abbot Basil Hume on 3 April 1963 what had only recently been termed the wind of change was already blowing through the monastery, schools and parishes. The most obvious differences, because most externally noticeable, were new ideas and new practices in the liturgy. But already what was later to become a numbers game was beginning to show. Priests were getting older, vocations were fewer, losses were occurring, and the pattern of parish life was changing. These belong to the history of the Church, but they provided the ground, and the challenge, which allowed Hume's qualities to emerge.[14]

As teacher, Hume was also a life-long learner, which enabled him to lead others. Hume was a leader of pilgrims, ever learning with them and from them. He knew he 'could never be a teacher without being a learner—and leaders must always be learners.'[15]

While serving a second term as Abbot, Hume was appointed ninth Archbishop of Westminster in February 1976, by Pope

Paul VI. In May of the same year, he was created Cardinal. In the sermon that he preached after his elevation to the See of Westminster was announced, he expressed his love and gratitude for the Ampleforth Community (monks, students, and parents) with words of encouragement:

> What has happened to me must happen to you. I have been raised to higher things in spite of myself; you, too, must be raised to higher things in spite of yourselves. So pause to think; let there be only noble thoughts in your minds, and noble deeds in your actions—let there be nothing mean or petty. The eyes of millions are on you as well as on me, for you are Ampleforth, and I am only moving to Westminster because I have been Abbot of Ampleforth.[16]

Hume anticipated the challenges and responsibilities that came with being the leader of the Catholic Church in England and Wales. In the address he gave in Westminster Cathedral on the day of his installation as Archbishop, he made an appeal to those under his care while revealing his character:

> At the outset of my ministry I ask you for your prayers, your understanding and your help. To remind myself constantly of the Christian calling I share with you all, and to be enlightened and strengthened to carry out with my brother-bishops the role entrusted to us of leadership and animation. And I put before you today a single appeal. Listen to the call of the Holy Spirit. The call today is clear. It is the call to holiness—to be first-rate in all we do, not second-rate. We are called to be men and women of integrity. We are called to be fully human—and, dare we say it, more than human, for we are called to share in the very life of God through the mystery of Christ's redeeming action. Here lies the secret. It is to recognise that God loves each one of us and that the strength of this love makes us bigger than we know ourselves to be, makes us Christ-like. It is a call to each of us as Christians. May we respond together in total generosity.[17]

Hume continued to challenge the faithful to respond to the call to holiness, that is, to be first-rate Christians. Well into his time as Archbishop, he addressed some of the problems inherent in a society in need of evangelization: 'Part of the problem is that many of our Catholics have received the sacraments, however infrequently, but have never been brought to the point of making a personal commitment to Christ. As we sometimes express it, too many people have been "sacramentalised" but not "evangelised". We cannot ignore the problem they present.'[18] He added,

> What is needed is not evangelisation in the strict sense of a first proclamation of the Gospel, but a more vigorous catechesis so radical and so sustained that it might be called a continuing evangelisation. We must constantly challenge the faithful—including ourselves—with the person and the message of Jesus Christ, with the fulness of the Word of God. Faith has to be deepened, strengthened, made more mature.[19]

His real challenge for continuing evangelization came two years before being appointed Archbishop when he posed a question to his monks: 'What part does the person of Jesus Christ play in my spiritual life?'[20] And he added, by way of explanation: 'I am talking about a personal relationship with Him.'[21] The relationship 'has to be one of intimacy and depth. We need also to discover that He is the way to Our Father, that he is the Father's way to us. There has to be a growing conviction that salvation comes from Him and through Him: that He is the very life of our souls.'[22] This is the challenge offered by Basil Hume to all the faithful.

As Archbishop in the late twentieth century, he prepared the faithful for the celebration of the millennium. He focused on a passage from the Gospel of Luke: 'All eyes in the synagogue were fixed on Him' (Lk 4:20). Hume exhorted believers:

> All our eyes should be fixed on Him, and if they are not then our celebration of the millennium will be an empty celebration, because the whole point of celebrating the

year 2000 is to remember that Jesus became man—God became man. That is the good news by which we must live and which, by our example, we share with other people. The very centre of our lives has to be Jesus Christ, true God and true man.[23]

He looked forward to welcoming the millennium and according to friend and colleague Cardinal Carlo Maria Martini, Hume had the gifts to do it: 'When I ask myself what qualities a bishop should have as we approach the new millennium, I see them embodied in Cardinal Hume.'[24] It was not God's plan for Hume to make it to the new millennium. In 1999, he was diagnosed with inoperable stomach cancer. He died on 17 June 1999, at the age of 76.

The Spirituality of Basil Hume

While an abbot and archbishop, Basil Hume's teachings and writings were not those of a scholastic or speculative theologian like Karl Rahner or Yves Congar. He was not a scholastic, but a monastic theologian. His faith and spirituality came quite naturally and created a tapestry comprised of the threads which constitute the spiritual life. It was important for Hume 'that minds and hearts should be involved in that search for God, where the seeking and the finding go hand in hand ... the process of getting to know God and learning to love Him.'[25] For Hume, the spiritual life was not something separate from the rest of one's life. For a definition of the spiritual life, he took a quotation from a work by Evelyn Underhill, which demonstrates such an all-encompassing and undivided life:

> What then, is the spiritual life? It is that interior life whereby I strive to encounter God and develop my relationship with Him by becoming increasingly more aware of Him and by desiring Him more intensely. It is not something separate from the rest of my life, a part of

me having no connection with anything else. The spiritual
life involves all that I do, all that happens to me; all that I
am; it should permeate every activity and be itself active at
every moment. It is furthermore the reason for my service
of God and neighbour. It is what makes me 'tick'. A spiritual
life is simply a life in which all we do comes from the centre
where we are anchored in God: a life soaked through and
through by a sense of His reality and claim, and self-given
to the great movement of His will.[26]

Hume was a model of the all-encompassing spiritual life, as
noted by a nephew who referred to his uncle by his baptismal name: 'There wasn't a spiritual George and a day-to-day
George. The two just were one, of a piece. That was the way he
came across.'[27]

Hume left part of himself in what he created, that is, his conferences, homilies and reflections delivered both within the monastic cloister and outside its confines, and in the relationships he
established with a wide variety of people. Something Pope St
John Paul II said about the nature of the artist in his 1999 *Letter
to Artists* can be said about Basil Hume: 'Not all are called to be
artists in the specific sense of the term. Yet, as Genesis has it,
all men and women are entrusted with the task of crafting their
own life: in a certain sense, they are to make of it a work of art,
a masterpiece.'[28] One will find similar words written by scholar
and philosopher A. K. Coomaraswamy who wrote, 'The artist is
not a special kind of man, but every man is a special kind of artist.'[29] Hume was a special kind of artist as monk, teacher, pastor,
preacher, and pilgrim. He crafted his own life and had the gift of
communicating the things of God to the People of God, believers and non-believers alike. Quite simply, yet profoundly, Basil
Hume gave others a glimpse of God. After Hume's death, Peter
Stanford spoke of Hume's 'greatest gift', namely, 'the boundless
capacity to recognize and nurture in others and in society at large
the spirituality and personal relationship with God that he so
patently carried within himself.'[30]

The work of art which Hume created was shaped and moulded first by prayer. He embodied what he taught: 'a man of prayer equals a man of God; and a man of God equals a man of spiritual influence.'[31] Although not a speculative theologian like Aquinas, Hume was like the Aquinas described by his contemporary, the Dominican scholar Paul Murray. Murray describes Aquinas as 'a theologian of prayer … a man of prayer';[32] so too was Basil Hume. Hume's monastic spirituality was rooted in the search for God through prayer, work, and community life. His main purpose throughout his monastic and extra-monastic life was the 'main purpose' of the monk, namely, 'to seek God' which 'he takes on as a life-long task.'[33]

Hume's work of art was also formed by lived experience or what W. H. Principe called the 'first level' of spirituality, that is, 'the *real* or *existential* level. This is a quality—the *lived* quality—of a person, as when we speak of the spirituality of St Benedict or St Francis or St Teresa of Avila. It is the way a person, within his or her historical and social context, understood and lived an ideal that was open and sensitive to the realm of the spirit, the transcendent, the other.'[34] Hume, open to the working of the Holy Spirit in his life, did not develop a system for the spiritual life, rather, he provided the tools for one who wishes to grow in spiritual maturity. He was familiar with the concepts of monastic teaching and living the Gospel of Jesus Christ whereby he spoke of the spiritual life with ease and comfortableness. A monk of Ampleforth commented: 'Basil's own approach to spirituality as well as to lots of other things was very non-systematic … he acted a lot on impulse and he expressed himself largely informally.'[35] Hume was also familiar with the writings of the English Mystics whose influence is felt throughout the English Benedictine Congregation (EBC). His confrère and historian Bernard Green writes:

> The EBC derived its spiritual outlook as well as its practical
> organisation and intellectual standing from the example and

inspiration of the Cassinese and Spanish Congregations.
They belonged to a fifteenth-century reform, with a great
emphasis on private prayer, spiritual reading and silence.
But the EBC also inherited the tradition of the fourteenth-
century English mystics, and preserved their teaching on
prayer and the spiritual life for posterity. The greatest
English spiritual writer since the Reformation, the man
who rediscovered the English mystics and blended their
teaching with that of the sixteenth- and seventeenth-century
French and Spanish writers and the fourteenth-century
Rhineland mystics, was a Benedictine, Augustine Baker.[36]

Hume's favourite English mystics included Julian of Norwich
(1342–1416) and the anonymous author of the *Cloud of Unknowing* (from the fourteenth century). In a conference to the monks
just after he deferred to Mother Julian's articulation of the love
of God: '"The love of God most high for our soul is so wonderful that it surpasses all knowledge"',[37] Hume encouraged the
Community to look to the English Mystics for guidance: 'That
mystical English tradition, I like to think, was influential at the
time of the re-foundation of our Congregation, and it has such
a marvellous relevance to what people are seeking today that
we would do well to read and follow this teaching, and acquire
something of this outlook.'[38] In a non-systematic way, he referred
not only to the English mystics but also to another favourite,
Thérèse of Lisieux (1873–97). His attraction to the Little Flower
may be related to what Dominic Milroy called 'the ordinariness
of his temperament and spirituality',[39] adding, 'Basil didn't have
a great system of spirituality and had no particular preference for
different styles of spirituality.'[40] On one occasion, Basil Hume
combined the *Cloud of Unknowing* and St Thérèse to suggest a
motto for the novitiate: 'Confidence: a boundless trust in God's
goodness. Yearning love: the love for God which is the point of
monastic life.'[41] He also found an etching in Thérèse of Lisieux's
cell particularly meaningful: '"*Jésus est mon unique amour*—Jesus
is my only love."'[42]

Basil Hume's schooling in the theological discipline of Thomism combined with the influence of the English mystics provided
the foundation whereby he could be spontaneous and impulsive,
trusting his intuition, addressing needs and issues as they arose
in a particular context. As a result, he had an ability to relate to
those with whom he came into contact. Not a pedant, he had the
gift of bringing his words to life and making them relevant and
accessible to the listener. The spiritual life is not a technique or
skill to be methodically acquired. The student of the spiritual life
strives to learn the various threads of the tapestry 'early on, but the
process of learning goes right on through life.'[43] Although refer-
ring to the 'difficult' and 'noble' art of schoolmastering, Hume's
wisdom applies to the spiritual life. The difficulty in learning
an art lies in the 'extent that we must be beginners all the time',
and the beginner learns 'in part from experience, in part from
those who have already had experience.'[44] As St Benedict wrote
a little rule for beginners,[45] so Basil Hume created a tapestry
of the spiritual life for beginners which is organic, flexible, and
suitable for all who seek union with God. While learning from
others, students of the spiritual life pray for the gift of grace so as
to be transformed, healed, and guided on the life-long journey to
God. The engagement of Hume's fundamental gift of faith with
his spirituality is a valuable guide for all those who seek the God
who loves them.

A Holy Man

When addressing fellow bishops, Basil Hume echoed the appeal
he made to all Christians on the day of his installation, namely, to
respond to the call to holiness: 'A bishop is expected to be holy.
That is rather frightening. Our people expect us to be men of God,
and the failure of our performance to match their expectations is
one of the burdens that we have to carry.'[46] He then listed 'three
qualities in holy people': First, 'they have discovered the love of

God and responded to it. The test that this love is authentic is the manner whereby it overflows into the world around them, their neighbours, but quite especially those who are in need and perhaps the most neglected.'[47] Second, 'they have an unbounded confidence in God and His providence, trusting Him with a trust which may seem at times almost unreasonable.'[48] Third, 'they have a certain positive zest for life. Very holy people are never bored, never cynical, never unkind, never bigotedly critical. They have a zest for life.'[49]

Was Basil Hume a holy man? To answer that question, it is helpful to quote people who knew him. Let us turn to a homily preached at a Requiem Mass by the then Abbot of Ampleforth, Timothy Wright (1942–2018). In this homily we find wonderfully articulated what might be called the secret behind the profound spiritual impact he made on so many people. Wright recalled:

> My lasting memory of Cardinal Basil occurred about six weeks ago. The cancer had been diagnosed but the effects were still relatively minor, hardly disrupting his schedule. We sat and talked after supper and then he said, I get very tired now and go to bed early. But next morning he was up early, at prayer, in his private chapel. That was his secret.[50]

Determined prayer was the secret to Hume's success:

> He was determined to give time to God every morning, every day, even to the extent of dragging an exhausted and decaying body out of bed. This makes it sound so easy; and at one level it is. You do not require a degree in spirituality, nor a stunning religious experience before you can start. You just have to be determined, determined to give time to God every day.[51]

Bishop John Crowley recalled:

> In Archbishop's House, Westminster, he would speak of 'going up to my cell' as he climbed the stairs to where his private apartment was on the top floor. Those deeply

ingrained habits of contemplation and prayer, the monastic rule, the re-forming of his entire being during those comparatively hidden (albeit intensely busy) years at Ampleforth were surely the key to everything else.[52]

Hume had discovered the love of God through prayer and responded to it, qualities of a holy man.

What were the results of his life of unceasing prayer? As Wright put it: 'It was these years of persevering prayer, early each morning which brought him face to face with his own weaknesses. He learnt he had to depend on God. He lived the apparent contradiction of experiencing his incompetence while becoming more clear-sighted about the ultimate goal.'[53] Although a man of trust, Basil Hume did doubt. As related by his nephew, Hume said: 'Nothing in my spiritual life do I find harder than to trust … I don't trust God enough. I do fret. I do fall into the trap of thinking that it all depends on "me".'[54] He grew in his trust of God as a holy person does, learning to trust Him with a trust which may at times seem unreasonable, as he stated: 'There was a time when I used to try to get rid of the anxieties and doubts, a time when I used to look for certainty. Then I realized: No, what matters is to trust God. Trusting God means throwing the whole thing into his hands.'[55]

Still, Basil Hume's perseverance in prayer was, as Wright called it, 'the seedbed into which he received the gift of humility.'[56] Wright called humility 'a gift, not a technique, and it grows on the back of helplessness.'[57] Hume used these words: 'Most people are only too aware that they have failed to achieve the ideal. Failure, like restlessness, can also be a friend, for its role is to introduce us to humility. Humility is facing up to reality, that is, to the truth about ourselves our sinfulness and limitations.'[58] His experiences of weakness, failure, doubt, and helplessness helped him be open to grace whereby he received the gift of humility, which, if judged by its fruits, found expression in Hume in the following ways: sense of humour and zest for life; giving of himself; authority; rootedness.

A Sense of Humour and a Zest for Life

Basil Hume had a sense of humour. Wright called it 'self-deprecating humour, the humour that was so much a part of him. He never took himself too seriously; there was always a twinkle in his eye. This made him accessible to us.'[59] That twinkle is a mark of one who is never bored and has a zest for life, both qualities of a holy person. David Goodall at the Requiem Mass at Blackfriars, Oxford, attested to his humour: 'As well as being endowed with a natural presence and dignity, he was helped by having the instincts, sense of timing and self-deprecating wit of an accomplished actor.'[60] Relating a story told to him by a confrère of Hume's, when Hume 'was a guest speaker at a dinner at the Inns of Court',[61] Goodall said, 'He was preceded by a distinguished judge, whose performance was so scintillating that it seemed doubtful if the Cardinal could match it. He rose to his feet, and after a short pause began: "I feel like a mongrel which has strayed into Cruft's".'[62] Hume's confrère Matthew Burns told this same story while including Hume's capacity to add 'that human touch, a little joke at his own expense.'[63] He commented on the audience's reaction to Hume's joke: 'There was shocked silence and they roared with laughter and he had them absolutely eating out of his own hand. It was a joke at his own expense, in a sense, but he made the point. That was one of his great gifts I think.'[64]

Hume's zest for life is revealed in the following story told by a friend and former student who taught him 'the art of throwing frisbees ... a deeply serious, almost religious activity in the early seventies'.[65] As related: '[Hume] became one on my best students, even getting quite good at it! When I was working in Tanzania he wrote to me complaining that since I left, his frisbee clientele was getting rather limited, but adding: "I have initiated at least three bishops to the noble art and have discovered that the Frisbee bounces uncommonly well off the throne floor!"'[66]

Basil Hume's zest for life was also exhibited by his commitment to physical fitness, related by a personal secretary:

Those first years at Westminster also had their fair share of sporting activity. It was a common occurrence for the track-suited archbishop and secretary to slip away to Battersea Park in mid-afternoon for a jog, or even for a rather vigorous running on the athletics track. As a variation, and sometimes quite late in the evening after a full day, there were visits to a local squash club. An energy sapping half-hour on court was then perfectly complemented by a subsequent swim. The gradual closing down of such pursuits as a hip joint rapidly deteriorated was a costly diminishment.[67]

It was no secret that Basil Hume was also a die-hard fan of New-castle United Football Club and a great admirer of Newcastle star Jackie Milburn (1924–88). As his confrère Bonaventure Knollys rightly said: 'He had an interest in sport, whatever it was. Perhaps it came across more noticeably because you don't expect it in bishops.'[68]

Giving of Himself

Hume gave of himself. Wright said, 'Humility empowered him to give himself to all of us especially the weak and the vulnerable. He was not embarrassed or ill at ease to come alongside us.'[69] His love of God overflowed to the world around him, a fruit of humility and a quality of a holy person. Kevin Nichols affirms this fruit in him: 'This acknowledgment of occasional bewilder-ment, lostness, vulnerability, proved in the long run to be one of his greatest strengths. People felt that he did not speak to them from a pinnacle but shared and understood their rather rickety lives. It was a rare and refreshing quality.'[70] Hume called this compassion: 'In practice we have to learn to be compassionate when we are young … to be concerned for the old, concerned for the sick, concerned for the handicapped, concerned for the poor, for the marginal. They are not "over there" but probably next door or in the home.'[71]

Authority

Hume spoke with authority. Timothy Wright stated: 'Because he was humble his teaching carried authority. Always loyal to his faith and obedient to the Church, he had that inner freedom, the mark of true obedience.'[72] As David Hope put it: '[Hume] knew the art of when to speak and when to keep silent—mostly keeping silent—so that when he did speak out it was with care, with discernment and with considerable authority.'[73] At his funeral Mass, the homilist said: 'For here was a monk, a bishop, who touched peoples' lives deep deep down because he knew God. Because he first inhabited his words, what he then said about God rang true. It had authority behind it. He spoke to us, as someone said, from the inside out.'[74] A confrère said:

> Basil Hume became, I would have thought, extraordinarily human precisely because he wasn't being pushed by other people. He had a spiritual message that he was giving to people that were going to be confirmed, ordained, or whatever it may be, parish visits, and all that ... He had enormous influence. He would have taken that without worrying what people would say. He only would have done that if he saw it was absolutely a question of principle. And again, he retained his humanity.[75]

Hume's secretary for twenty-one years, provides a fitting summary of his authority: 'He was a mystical soul who reminded us all that we are made for the vision of God. To see Him as He is, face to face. A vision I am sure he is enjoying to the full.'[76]

Rootedness

Hume was rooted. Timothy Wright said: 'Humility both rooted him in this world, but separated him from it. Always at heart the committed monk, he grew into that wonderful human being, now widely respected, a true example of how living closely with Christ improves and enriches human nature'[77] Bishop Brian Noble adds: 'I think the thing that I would say right from the very beginning, all of us, as bishops, would say, Basil never ceased to be a monk. In spite of becoming an archbishop and a cardinal and being a highly influential member of the Church at a high level so to speak, he was still very much the monk'[78]

Hume lived closely with Christ and was not only enriched himself, but he enriched others. A few examples—Member of Parliament Ann Widdecombe: 'Holiness can bring unworldliness and detach the holy from the world but along with great spirituality Cardinal Hume emanates approachability and humanity';[79] Dame Joanna Jamieson: 'He was a real person to me. When he appeared at any monastic event, he just wore his black habit. It was very impressive. The Cardinal was coming, and he just walked in. Sometimes people who do that, you feel they're making a statement but you didn't feel that with him. He was just being himself';[80] Hume's successor at Westminster, Cardinal Cormac Murphy-O'Connor (1932–2017): 'Basil was very good with people. He started where they were. It might be talking about football, or talking about anything else. People found that very endearing … He had a great way with young people. That was a quality I think he used, but it was very, very effective in terms of making people, especially young people, at ease with him, which is a human quality, but also a spiritual one.'[81]

Two other examples of Basil Hume's ability to enrich others revolve around his ability to discern a Benedictine vocation, telling of his care for those that others might dismiss. One monk, Cyprian Smith, shared the story of when he asked to join the monastery. Smith was considered old (turning 30), he was disabled, and the Community thought they would not get any work out of him. Hume did not agree. As Smith put it:

> [Hume] said, yes, he's disabled and he's not young, but he's not all that disabled, and he's not all that old. I would

reckon we'll have about fifteen years work out of him
before he needs to be in a wheelchair. But I think even if
we had to keep him in a wheelchair all his life, I think we
should still take him. So, it was passed that I was allowed
to do the novitiate. They've had more than fifteen years
actually; I'm actually still working![82]

With realism, Smith added:

He had a certain skill in discernment. He could tell,
sometimes at a glance, whether a person had a religious
vocation to the Benedictine life, or not ... Not always. But
there was as if there was a window that opened up in his
mind and he saw something. It didn't work with everybody
but it did with some and sometimes he just didn't know
any more than anybody else did but other times he had
kind of an intuitive certainty about a certain individual
and was proved right in every case I've heard.[83]

Basil Hume's first novice, Edgar Miller, shared the story of his
entrance into Ampleforth which started under Abbot Byrne.
Miller related:

When the council met, Abbot Byrne sent me a letter saying
they decided to defer my entry. So, I wasn't entirely, terribly
pleased with that. He had actually asked me to get sorted
out to come in the September. However, knowing the way
we do with St Benedict and his Rule, I kept knocking at the
door. And there was to be an abbatial election that coming
year. The Community decided to have another Abbot,
and it was Basil Hume. Basil Hume knew about my case
because he had been on the council. He wrote me a very
lovely letter and said, come up for my blessing. I arrived
at his blessing and he said there's no question about your
entry, you're coming, come what may, even if the council
have other reservations. You're coming. So, I came. And
he was marvellous. I was one of eight in the novitiate and
I'm the only one left![84]

Reflection

In an address previously videotaped then delivered to the United States Bishops' Conference the day after he died, Basil Hume made one last appeal for the primacy of prayer: 'All of us in the Church must become more deeply spiritual. Prayer is a priority for all of us. Today people are crying out to be taught how to pray and to be given a deeper meaning of what life is about. People are looking for spirituality.'[85] Emphasizing his beliefs by way of personal experience, he stated, 'A few years ago I had to give an important talk to a large number of top professionals, company directors and the like. The topic they requested was "Spirituality and Morality."'[86] He stressed, 'That is the need today. People want to hear about God and to hear about their relationship with Him.'[87] Such is the work of evangelization as expressed by Pope Paul VI:

> The world which, paradoxically, despite innumerable signs of the denial of God, is nevertheless searching for Him in unexpected ways and painfully experiencing the need of Him—the world is calling for evangelizers to speak to it of a God whom the evangelists themselves should know and be familiar with as if they could see the invisible. The world calls for and expects from us simplicity of life, the spirit of prayer, charity towards all, especially towards the lowly and the poor, obedience and humility, detachment and self-sacrifice. Without this mark of holiness, our word will have difficulty in touching the heart of modern man. It risks being vain and sterile.[88]

In response to the Holy Father's exhortation, Hume encouraged the American bishops:

> We want our people to walk as if they could see the invisible and to have fallen in love with God. The pilgrim people of God, journeying into the next millennium, must meet again that pilgrim coming in the opposite direction, Him

who is the Way, the Truth, and the Life, whom to see is to have seen the Father. Christ must be born afresh into our world.[89]

Hume identified genuine sincerity as the quality of a person who lives in close contact with Christ the Lord. In the chapters that follow, he speaks as monk, pastor, and preacher. He speaks as a man of manifest sincerity, and as one in love with Christ the Lord. Throughout his life, marked by the desire for holiness, he was able, in many of the words he spoke, to touch minds and hearts like few others of his generation.

NOTES

[1]   Hume, *To Be a Pilgrim: A Spiritual Notebook*, p. 217.

[2]   Charles, ed., *Basil Hume: Ten Years*, p. 14.

[3]   *Ibid.*

[4]   M. Craig, 'The Early Years', in T. Castle, ed., *Basil Hume: A Portrait* (London: Fount, 1987), p. 29.

[5]   Hume in J. Mortimer, *In Character: Interviews with Some of the Most Influential and Remarkable Men and Women of Our Time* (New York: Penguin Books, 1984), p. 89.

[6]   D. Milroy, 'Hume the Abbot, 1963–1976', in C. Butler, ed., *Basil Hume: by his Friends* (London: Fount, 1999), p. 10.

[7]   D. Milroy, interview by author, Ampleforth Abbey, York, 9 September 2013.

[8]   Milroy, 'Hume the Abbot, 1963–1976', p. 11.

[9]   *Ibid.*

[10]   B. Hume, *Searching for God* (New York: Paulist Press, 1978), p. 11.

[11]   B. Hume, unpublished conference, 18 December 1964, used with permission of the Ampleforth Abbey Trust, York.

[12]   Hume, *Searching for God*, p. 13.

[13]   *Ibid.*

[14]   A. Cramer, *Ampleforth: The Story of St Laurence's Abbey and College*, Saint Laurence Papers V (Ampleforth Abbey: Ampleforth Abbey Trustees, 2001), p. 177.

[15]   B. Hume, *Cardinal Basil Hume: In My Own Words*, ed. T. de Bertodano (London: Hodder & Stoughton, 1999), p. 83.

[16]   Hume, 'Sermon delivered by Father Abbot at the Sunday Mass of 22nd February 1976, six days after the announcement of his elevation to the See of Westminster', in Hume, *Searching for God*, p. 191.

[17] B. Hume, 'Address in Westminster Cathedral on the Day of Hume's Installation, March 25, 1976', *The Tablet* (3 April 1976), p. 348.

[18] Hume, *To Be a Pilgrim*, p. 181.

[19] *Ibid.*, pp. 181–182.

[20] Hume, *Searching for God*, p. 186.

[21] *Ibid.*

[22] *Ibid.*, p. 187.

[23] B. Hume, *The Mystery of the Incarnation* (Brewster, MA: Paraclete Press, 2000), p. 3.

[24] C. M. Martini, 'A Boon to Us All', in Butler, ed., *Basil Hume: By his Friends*, p. 78.

[25] B. Hume, *Basil in Blunderland* (Brewster, MA: Paraclete Press, 1999), p. xi.

[26] E. Underhill in B. Hume, *Towards a Civilization of Love: Being Church in Today's World* (London: Hodder & Stoughton, 1995), p. 99.

[27] P. Westmacott, interview by author, Ampleforth Abbey, York, 22 September 2013.

[28] Pope St John Paul II, *Letter of His Holiness Pope John Paul II to Artists* (4 April 1999).

[29] A. K. Coomaraswamy, *The Transformation of Nature in Art* (New York: Dover Publications, 1934), p. 64.

[30] P. Stanford, *Cardinal Hume and the Changing Face of English Catholicism* (London: Geoffrey Chapman, 1999), p. viii.

[31] Hume, *Searching for God*, p. 119.

[32] P. Murray, *Praying with Confidence: Aquinas on the Lord's Prayer* (London: Continuum, 2010), p. 4.

[33] Hume, *Searching for God*, p. 14.

[34] W. H. Principe, 'Thomas Aquinas' Spirituality', in *The Gilson Lectures on Thomas Aquinas: With an Introduction by James P. Reilly*. Étienne Gilson Series 30 (Toronto, Ontario, Canada: Pontifical Institute of Mediaeval Studies, 2008), p. 181.

[35] Milroy, interview by author.

[36] B. Green, *The English Benedictine Congregation: A Short History* (London: Catholic Truth Society, n.p.), p. 19.

[37] Julian of Norwich in Hume, *Searching for God*, p. 88.

[38] Hume, *Searching for God*, p. 88.

[39] Milroy, interview by author.

[40] *Ibid.*

[41] Hume, *Searching for God*, p. 27.

[42] B. Hume, *The Mystery of Love* (Brewster, MA: Paraclete Press, 2001), p. 39.

[43] Hume, unpublished conference, 19 January 1964.

[44]   Hume, *Searching for God*, p. 95.

[45]   See *The Rule of St Benedict*, 73:8.

[46]   B. Hume, *Light in the Lord: Reflections on Priesthood* (repr. Collegeville: Liturgical Press, 1993), p. 150.

[47]   *Ibid.*

[48]   *Ibid.*

[49]   *Ibid.*

[50]   T. Wright, 'Praying before God' Requiem Mass for Cardinal Basil Hume, Ampleforth Abbey, 19 June 1999, in P. Walesby and M. Webster, eds., *Homilies Given at the Funeral Rites of Cardinal George Basil Hume, OSB, OM* (London: Abbeyville Printing, n.d.), p. 22.

[51]   *Ibid.*

[52]   J. Crowley, Middlesbrough Diocese Requiem Mass, 22 June 1999, Middlesbrough Cathedral, Middlesbrough, in unpublished booklet, used with permission of the Ampleforth Abbey Trust, p. 5.

[53]   Wright, 'Praying before God,' pp. 22–3.

[54]   Hume in Charles, ed., *Basil Hume: Ten Years On*, p. 191.

[55]   Hume, *The Mystery of Love*, p. 40.

[56]   Wright, 'Praying before God,' p. 23.

[57]   *Ibid.*

[58]   Hume, *The Mystery of Love*, p. 32.

[59]   Wright, 'Praying before God,' p. 24.

[60]   D. Goodall, Requiem Mass, 16 October 1999, Blackfriars Oxford, in unpublished booklet, p. 14.

[61]   *Ibid.*

[62]   *Ibid.*

[63]   M. Burns, interview by author, Ampleforth Abbey, York, 16 September 2013.

[64]   *Ibid.*

[65]   S. King, Ampleforth Abbey Memorial Vespers, 16 October 1999, Ampleforth Abbey, York, in unpublished booklet, p. 20.

[66]   *Ibid.*

[67]   J. Crowley, 'The First Years at Westminster', in Butler, ed., *Basil Hume: By his Friends*, pp. 37–8.

[68]   B. Knollys, interview by author, Ampleforth Abbey, York, 20 September 2013.

[69]   Wright, 'Praying before God,' p. 24.

[70]   K. Nichols, *Pilgrimage of Grace: Cardinal Basil Hume, 1923–1999* (Dublin: Veritas, 2000), p. 14.

[71]   Hume, *Cardinal Basil Hume: In My Own Words*, p. 103.

[72] Wright, 'Praying before God,' p. 24.

[73] D. Hope, 'Memorial Vespers' 16 October 1999, Ampleforth Abbey, York, in unpublished booklet, pp. 8–9.

[74] J. Crowley, 'Homily at Funeral Mass' 25 June 1999 in Walesby and Webster, eds., *Homilies Given at the Funeral Rites of Cardinal George Basil Hume, OSB, OM*, p. 18.

[75] Knollys, interview by author.

[76] S. McAllister, 'Colleague and Friend', in Charles, ed., *Basil Hume: Ten Years On*, p. 111.

[77] Wright, 'Praying before God,' p. 24.

[78] B. Noble, interview by author, Pontifical Beda College, Rome, Italy, 11 November 2013.

[79] A. Widdecombe, 'Holiness and Hassle', in Butler, ed., *Basil Hume: By his Friends*, p. 84.

[80] J. Jamieson, nun of Stanbrook, interview by author, Stanbrook Abbey, 13 September 2013.

[81] C. Murphy-O'Connor, interview by author, Venerable English College, Rome, Italy, 29 November 2013.

[82] C. Smith, interview by author, Ampleforth Abbey, York, 21 September 2013.

[83] *Ibid.*

[84] E. Miller, interview by author, Ampleforth Abbey, York, 18 September 2013.

[85] B. Hume, 'A Bishop's Relation to the Universal Church and His Fellow Bishops', *Origins* 29/7 (1 July 1999), p. 112.

[86] *Ibid.*

[87] *Ibid.*

[88] Pope Paul VI, Apostolic Exhortation *Evangelii Nuntiandi*, 76.

[89] Hume, 'A Bishop's Relation to the Universal Church and His Fellow Bishops', p. 112.

Chapter 2

Hume the Monk

B ASIL HUME delivered conferences to his monks weekly and
at what he called 'special monastic "moments",'[1] namely,
times 'when the Abbot was required to speak to his monks
... known as "Chapter".'[2] These conferences speak highly of the
solid spiritual formation the monks received throughout their
monastic life. Hume spoke to the entire Community assembled
in the choir during special monastic moments. The occasion
may be for Clothing, Profession, or Perseverance, yet the whole
Community, no doubt with varying levels of attention, were
present for Hume's teaching. Hume's message was a means for
both initial formation and on-going formation; a wise approach
for any abbot. Hume passed on the spiritual tradition, a tradition
that is purely monastic, purely Benedictine, and purely character-
istic of the Ampleforth Community. As a result, individual and
communal spirituality becomes almost palpable. No one need
question what it means to be a Benedictine monk of Ampleforth.

When Archbishop of Westminster, Hume delivered talks during the year-long celebration of the 1500th anniversary of the birth
of St Benedict. From 21 March 1980 until 21 March 1981, Hume,
'the only Benedictine in the College of Cardinals',[3] delivered
talks around the world on St Benedict and the Rule 'under very
different circumstances and to very different audiences.'[4] In these
talks, Hume showed how his Benedictine spirituality matured
during his years as Cardinal Archbishop.

The spirituality of Benedictine life as articulated by Hume is
rich, diverse and practical, covering themes of Benedictine for-

mation, Benedictine living, and Benedictine renewal. To give his
spirituality a specific focus, these themes will be treated under
the image of *arts*, a word Hume used in different, evocative ways.
This approach enables a new insight into Benedictine spirituality,
one that is distinctively his. At a Clothing Chapter, Hume alerted
newcomers: 'there are three arts which you have to learn early
on, but the process of learning goes right through life.'[5] First,
'the art of seeking God's will', second, 'the art of being humble',
third, 'the art of prayer'.[6] On another occasion, Hume spoke of
the 'art of loving',[7] an 'art that needs to be learnt; its disciplines,
its limits, its constraints must be understood.'[8] Hume stressed
the importance of the art of loving: 'Discipline without love is
bleak; love without discipline is catastrophic—a disciplined love
is a power to achieve great and noble deeds.'[9]

Hume did not overlook the dimension of grace when learning
an art and putting it into practice. He emphasized: 'What you
have to learn is that each act of yours has to become an act of love:
your response in love to a love which has first been given to you',[10]
an echo of St Benedict: 'See how the Lord in his love shows us the
way of life.'[11] Learning an art and living it, then, is a response to
the gift of grace freely given by the Lord. Grace enables all those
interested in the teachings of St Benedict to 'progress in this way
of life and in faith, to run on the path of God's commandments,
our hearts overflowing with the inexpressible delight of love.'[12]
At a Solemn Profession Chapter, Hume emphasized the role of
grace in the Benedictine vocation: 'In the days which follow your
Profession I would recommend that you meditate on those words
of the Magnificat and recognize just what God will have achieved
in you in that ceremony, and with His grace will achieve in you
during the course of your monastic life.'[13] Learning the arts of
Benedictine spirituality as taught by Basil Hume, Benedictines
declare with St Paul: 'By God's grace I am what I am.'[14]

As abbot, Basil Hume taught the art of searching for God, a
rich and colourful tapestry comprised of various *arts*. These arts
constitute the spiritual life of all Christians, specifically here,

though, the Community at Ampleforth. Hume's teaching is sol-
idly grounded in Gospel values, Benedictine spirituality, and the
monastic tradition which makes it continually relevant. No matter
the venue or audience, Hume presented the art of searching for
God as realistic, uncomplicated, and pragmatic. It is the simple
message that can have the most impact, attested to by Hume in
an interview with John Mortimer: 'it's remarkable how many
people you can help by saying something quite simple.'[15] In its
simplicity and profundity, Hume's message was accessible to
all people, regardless of their state in life. As Hume wrote, 'The
principles which guide the monk in his search for God and the
Gospel values, which he tries to make his, are relevant to both
Christians and non-Christians alike',[16] whether one lives inside
or outside of the monastery.

The heart of Hume's message is that the whole of monastic
life is a journey, a life-long journey of learning and conversion
as a monk, yearning for everlasting life, searching for God in and
with a particular monastic community. The overarching arts of
his teaching are two-fold: First, the primary work of the Benedictine is the search for God. In a Clothing Chapter, he told those
entering the Community, 'If you are asked the question, "Why did
you come to the monastery?", the only valid answer is "To seek
God."'[17] Hume reinforced the primacy and constancy of the task:

> The monastic life is, above all else, a search for God. It
> is not the acquiring of virtues, or the fostering of moral
> integrity; it is not carrying the Cross, it is not going flat-
> out at work; it is not living obedience; it does not provide
> an environment for an individual to discover himself and
> work at his own spirituality. Any of these would constitute a
> partial vision of what monasticism is. They are component
> parts; but they are means, not ends. The end is the search
> for union with God.
> It is a search for God in community.[18]

Second is the art of charity. The crux of Hume's message was
delivered in one of the first addresses to the Community and

pointed to the conciliar call to the perfection of charity[19]: 'Our life is one of charity, the love of God and of our neighbour.'[20] Hume further clarified his thoughts on charity as he summed up the monastic life in one phrase: 'intimacy with God. That is what the whole thing leads to; another way of expressing the love of God, or the word "charity": "intimacy with God", to which all our activities lead and from which, of course, all those activities should flow.'[21] Hume taught charity as not only 'the love of God and of our neighbour',[22] but also as 'the service of God and the service of our neighbour',[23] which for Hume, was 'the monastic ideal.'[24] When reading Hume's words, then, one is focused on the monastic ideal and is able to reflect upon how a particular art leads to and flows from charity, what the Church calls a virtue, the one by which 'the practice of all the virtues is animated and inspired'.[25] The more intimate one is with the Lord, the more charitable he or she will be. Growing in charity, the seeker deepens intimacy with God, strengthens the relationship with the God who loves beyond measure, and grows in love and service of neighbour.

The life-long search for God through service of which Hume speaks requires energy—with enthusiasm, joy, openness, and enduring perseverance. Enthusiasm for the life is necessary, yet, as Hume made clear, it can be 'difficult to talk about because to some extent enthusiasm and its manifestations depend on temperament, and an artificial demonstration would be out of place.'[26] One must allow for varying degrees of enthusiasm and levels of energy, which often ebb and flow. Benedictines must allow others to be themselves while encouraging one another to strive for his or her best self. Hence, the wisdom of St Benedict when exhorting his followers to bear with one another in weakness of body and behaviour.[27]

Hume also insists on the importance of joy, no matter where one is on the spiritual journey. Speaking on the occasion of Renewal of Vows, he stressed: 'We should renew in ourselves the conviction that our life is worthwhile—not to be over-anx-

ious about exterior things but treasure our inner secret: union
with God and our brethren, in true charity. There must be joy in
our service of God (we have a right to this), a peace and serenity
which are signs of life with God.'[28] At Solemn Professions, Hume
addressed the monks about their constant search for God and
the approach needed:

> You are now beginning in earnest the lifelong task of
> searching for God ... as from tomorrow, you will commit
> yourselves to seek Him, seek Him above all, before all, Him
> alone. And that search will go on, day after day, month after
> month, year after year; never relenting, never becoming
> half-hearted, and never, above all, discouraged.[29]

Nine years later, Hume described the monastic life as 'an unre-
lenting, keen, joyful search for God',[30] a search which takes precedence over all other activities because, as Hume declared, 'Our
primacy is to seek the face of God in all circumstances, in all persons',[31] an echo of an earlier exhortation at a Solemn Profession:

> You have come here to seek God, and that is all you have
> come here for: everything else is incidental—in one sense;
> in another sense, everything is a means towards that. And
> you can rest assured that, if you take this life seriously,
> provided that you have good will, you will find God can
> be found in this life of ours, as it is lived here.[32]

Over and over again, Hume keeps the monks focused on the
primacy of the art of searching for God, but not without reason.
How easy it is to get weighed down with the demands of life,
which include, but are not limited to specific work assignments,
difficulties in relationships, disappointments, illness, struggles,
unrealized expectations, and frustrations, all of which can detract
from the impetus of the search for God, namely, that our constant search for God 'is only our way of expressing our response
to His search for us.'[33] To emphasize his point, Hume referred
the Community to the three parables in chapter 15 of St Luke's

Gospel: the woman who lost her coin (Lk 15:8–10), the lost sheep (Lk 15:1–7) and the prodigal son (Lk 15:11–32), what he called 'one of the profoundest illustrations of what the attitude of the Father is to us.'[34] So moving are those accounts, Hume added, 'it is difficult to read that Chapter and remain unaffected.'[35] The Father in His endless mercy, love, and tenderness continues His relentless search for us, drawing us ever closer to Him, whether we are lost in spiritual darkness, have drifted from the flock, or been wasteful and foolish.

Recognizing that God never wearies in His search for them, Benedictines must never grow weary in their search for God. This search is really the centre of the monastic vocation. Hume called the centre 'an exploration into the mystery which is God. A search for an experience of His reality',[36] which 'is a life-long enterprise.'[37] Hume added, 'what I am really saying is that it is on our part a response to an initiative that rests entirely with him.'[38] Hume summarizes the basis of monastic life, one of searching and responding, saying, 'Our monastic life must be based on an initial act of faith, an initial acceptance of God, and we spend the rest of our life trying to discover more about Him and to respond more completely as a result.'[39]

Hume shaped and moulded the Community at Ampleforth and any of those who received his teaching, while simultaneously giving his audience the freedom and responsibility to grow in their understanding and articulation of the spiritual life through the day-to-day living of the Benedictine Rule and Gospel values. Hume spoke of the relationship between knowledge gained from instruction and the lived experience at the time of a Simple Profession: 'You know the answers to a great number of questions which could be put to you concerning the vows. But you probably do not understand them yet, and this is the key to what I am trying to say at the moment. You have got to live them to understand them.'[40]

In his teaching, Hume brought the Rule to life. He reinforced and reaffirmed the values, attitudes, and actions to be inculcated

in every pilgrim learning the art of searching for God. Hume presented an authentic form of Benedictine life clarifying just what it
means to be Benedictine in any particular community, monastic
or otherwise, at any particular time in history. He presented an
art form which is Benedictine, for 'monasticism is a "way of life",
and the word "way" recalls the pilgrim character of this life and
of our monastic history.'41 Hume presents a way of life leading
to self-fulfilment, not the self-fulfilment 'which is self-seeking,
self-asserting, self-regarding,'42 but the 'self-fulfilment in the
monastic situation,'43 which is 'the by-product, or the happy
effect, of seeking God's will before all things. If you have this as
your programme for life then, inevitably, self-fulfilment—not the
kind that you may be dreaming of at the moment—will follow.'44
His message is relevant to any pilgrim in the school of the Lord's
service, or any committed Christian who seeks 'the Lord [who]
waits for us daily to translate into action, as we should, his holy
teachings'45 and desires to live out their baptismal call.

The Art of Monastic Instinct

As abbot, Hume spoke of religious instinct. As Hume put it:
'Man, I am convinced, is religious by nature. The religious instinct
belongs to his very nature, is part of his make-up. It is part of his
make-up to be oriented towards God.'46 Religious instinct then
directs the human person learning the art of searching for God.
There are also particular expressions of religious instinct. Some
expressions come naturally, for example, if a person is drawn
to the beauty of sacred music in the liturgy. For Hume, 'liturgy
should always contain within it the beautiful, because beauty is
one of the means by which we are led to God.'47 A person may be
drawn, then, to the beauty of Gregorian chant, which according
to the Second Vatican Council, should 'be given a place of primacy in liturgical activity.'48. If liturgy, as Hume stated, 'should
sometimes and in some circumstances deliberately speak to us of

God through beauty',[49] then the beauty of Gregorian chant can be something which 'activates the religious instinct',[50] leads us to God, and is 'one of the means whereby this instinct will find expression.'[51] One may also receive an expression of religious instinct as gift in the form of special graces 'intended for the common good of the Church',[52] for example, the gift of teaching, preaching, administration, or healing (see 1 Cor. 12:28).

Hume presented another expression of religious instinct, a specific instinct that is monastic, and one that guides a Benedictine's heart and directs his or her thoughts, words, and actions, both within the cloister and without. St Benedict succinctly presents the underlying premise for the actions of all monastics, and the abbot in particular: 'Your way of acting should be different from the world's way.'[53] The abbot 'must not show too great a concern for the fleeting and temporal things of this world, neglecting or treating lightly the welfare of those entrusted to him.'[54] It is not worldly cares or concerns that dominate the life of a Benedictine. Rather, 'the love of Christ must come before all else.'[55] St Benedict's terms are non-negotiable. It is the love of Christ and nothing else that compels the Benedictine to instinctively serve God and serve neighbour.

For Hume, monastic instinct 'is a kind of instinct by which one is able to judge what is fitting for a monk and what is not.'[56] Monastic instinct covers 'a wide spectrum of activity, speech, the way we pass our holidays, how we spend money, the kind of hospitality we give, the kind we receive, our behaviour, things we say, or values.'[57] There should be 'an awareness, within reach of us all, as to what is fitting and what is not.'[58] In other words, monastic instinct is pervasive. As the Benedictine grows in spiritual maturity, the awareness of appropriate behaviours and attitudes becomes sharper, more readily accessible as the days and years unfold. Provided the Benedictine is open to the work of the Holy Spirit and gives himself or herself entirely to the monastic life as lived in a particular community, they will develop a keen sense of the awareness that should guide life.

Although a person does not come to the monastery with a well-developed monastic instinct, she or he may have a propensity for such an instinct. Monastic instinct is an art in the sense that it needs to be developed and nurtured over time like any artistic gift. Hence the reason why Hume addresses its importance. A community must be reminded about matters of the heart and mind over and over again, as humans have short memories. Monastic instinct must be continuously cultivated.

The newcomer to monastic life first becomes aware of monastic instinct in the novitiate. St Benedict, when addressing the reception of newcomers to the monastery, describes the *novitiate* as a place 'where the novices study, eat and sleep.'[59] It is also a place where the novice 'should be exposed to all the trials of monastic life which appear to be hard and harsh but which lead us on our way to God.'[60] It is in the novitiate that monastic instinct is inculcated. The seeds of this art, the awareness of what is fitting and what is not, are planted and begin to sprout. A well-formed and deeply embedded monastic instinct protects from the lures of activism, at Ampleforth in the forms of its apostolic works of teaching, giving retreats, and parish obligations. Hume knew the dangers of the active life, where activity so easily supersedes the responsibility of prayer and commitment to community life. At Ampleforth, the novitiate provided an environment designed for the novice to learn responsibility and maturity in the development of this monastic instinct. Hume knew life in the novitiate was difficult; he wanted the newcomers to be prepared. Rightly, Hume described the novitiate as 'constricting and confining',[61] even 'unexciting, uneventful. Perhaps it is also bleak for considerable periods of time.'[62] At a Clothing Chapter, Hume invited the novices to look positively beyond the novitiate and its separation from the Community, saying 'you should begin now to feel yourselves to be part of a family which has much to give you and to which in increasing measure you will be expected to contribute.'[63] As a member of a monastic family, the novice learns to be a disciple, 'to learn quickly and surely the principles of the monastic life', for 'what really matters is achieving a monastic spirit.'[64] Monastic spirit includes exhibiting the fruits of the art of charity; joy, peace and mercy, as well as beneficence and benevolence.[65] Others should find those with monastic spirit and instinct 'easy, approachable, warm, but they should detect something else. It is a "something else" built up through the years of fidelity, striving, having one's treasure elsewhere.'[66] It is wisdom and insight gained through another art—that of prayer.

While growing into this monastic art, novices 'grow soon to monastic maturity,'[67] and learn 'to embrace those things which are going to lead you to God.'[68] The things which will lead one to God are learning to "become men of prayer, learn[ing] the art of prayer, learn[ing] the practice of the presence of God that you should become "men of God".'[69] While becoming men of God, becoming ever more aware of the presence of God, the novices nurture monastic instinct, the awareness of what is fitting and what is not so that they can best serve God and neighbour. Monastic instinct will guide how one thinks and behaves in the monastery, at work, in public, while on holiday. Hume reminded the monks 'that people look for, and expect to see in us, something different which can speak to them of God.'[70] Benedictines with monastic instinct radiate the qualities that draw others to God; they radiate the fruits of the Holy Spirit!

Key to developing monastic instinct, Hume believed, is for novices to be in an environment in which they are immersed into a life of prayer. Quickly, novices begin to grow as the foundations of the monastic instinct are inculcated. The result: they, with the community, can better discern 'whether it is God Himself that they truly seek, whether they have a real love for the work of God combined with a willing acceptance of obedience and of any demands on their humility and patience that monastic life may make on them',[71] which, according to St Benedict, are the criteria by which novices are judged.

If suited to monastic life, the novice grows into that life, draws from and becomes increasingly a witness to the monastic art.

God will intervene in the future Benedictine's life, gifting them with the actual graces[72] to fully embrace the monastic vocation to seek God. In all aspects of monastic life, the Benedictine becomes more and more adept at judging what is appropriate, and what is not.

The Art of Being Benedictine

Simply living in the monastery does not make a person a Benedictine, that is, one who does not 'get too involved in purely worldly affairs.'[73] Learning the art of being Benedictine can take many years, if not a lifetime. Where does one learn the art of being Benedictine? In the novitiate. Stressing the importance of the novitiate, Hume told novices: 'And I think that if you persevere and later in life look back, you will see, indeed understand, how formative this year can be, or was, or, sadly, was not. In this year the foundations are laid. In this year you have to become "monks" instead of just living like monks.'[74] As the seeds for monastic instinct are sown in the novitiate, so are the seeds for learning the art of being Benedictine.

In the introduction to his published Chapters, Hume posed the question, 'What is a monk?'[75] He called it a 'fair'[76] question but one to which 'no tidy definition can be given'.[77] No neat and clean definition can be given to an age-old question, oft debated in monastic circles due to the variety of lifestyles that Benedictines have lived throughout the centuries. 'In fact,' as Hume told those gathered at Ealing Abbey, 'there had been monks in the Church for two hundred years before St Benedict's time, and there were many Rules by which monks could live.'[78] The Rule that St Benedict created was adapted from the rules that preceded his. Another fact is that 'St Benedict did not mean to found an Order. In this he is unlike many later saints—such as St Francis or St Ignatius; nor did he intend to write the Rule for any save his own monks at Monte Cassino.'[79] Hume saw those facts as important in describing Benedictines, and therefore important in understanding what it means to be one. As Benedictines, he told the assembly: 'We do not see ourselves as having any particular mission or function in the Church. We do not set out to change the course of history. We are just there—almost by accident from a human point of view. And, happily, we go on "just being there".'[80] What are Benedictines, then? As Hume explained, they 'are ordinary people, on the whole. We are not spiritually star performers. So the Rule of St Benedict makes it possible for ordinary folk to live lives of quite extraordinary virtue.'[81]

Just being there, Benedictine men and women live according to the Latin adage *agere sequitur esse*, that is, they live in such a way where *doing* follows *being*—a life where the human person comes first, not his or her job titles or accomplishments. Focusing on the value of the human person, Hume stated, 'The Rule demands that monks be seen as individuals, each precious in the sight of God, and the Rule is full of compassion.'[82] As a compassionate leader, the abbot should focus on who community members are, not what they do. It is the abbot's job to respect the dignity of the human person and be concerned with the welfare of each individual. The abbot is to 'avoid all favouritism in the monastery',[83] and 'keep in mind that he has undertaken the care of souls for whom he must give an account.'[84] The abbot must yield to 'discretion, the mother of virtues,'[85] and 'be discerning and moderate'[86] in approach, and 'so arrange everything that the strong have something to yearn for and the weak nothing to run from.'[87]

Doing following being is not just for Benedictines, but for all Christians as stated by one of Hume's confrères: 'Our life as Christians is not about *doing* anything, but about *being* something. Once we understand, and start to become, what we are meant to be, then we have a much better chance of understanding and achieving what we are meant to do.'[88] The being aspect of Christian civilization is quite contrary to what one finds in the twenty-first century, where being follows doing. In St Benedict's vision, the stronger value is placed on the human person, not on what he or she does. Hume made this vision clear at a Clothing Chapter when he told newcomers, 'We do not take you into this Community because we think you are going to be useful to us; we do not take you on because we want your skill or your experience: we have taken you on because we think you are seeking God and we think that you will make good monks; that is what matters.'[89]

Instead of asking, 'What is a monk?', a better question may be, 'What kind of people should Benedictines be?' They are people who respond affirmatively to the Lord's invitation, 'Is there anyone here who yearns for life and desires to see good days?'[90] A Benedictine is 'anyone who leads a life without guile, who does what is right, who speaks truth from the heart, on whose tongue there is no deceit, who never harms a neighbour nor believes evil reports about another.'[91] From this we can see the inspiration of Hume's words in his address to Benedictine men and women at St Vincent Archabbey, USA, during which he said, 'We, monks and sisters, have an important, indeed a vital role to play in the life of the Church. We must speak to men and women of our society about God and the things of God, and this we shall do by living the Gospel and communicating it by our example, by our attitudes, by our teaching.'[92] The role then of the abbot, guardian and promoter of the Benedictine vocation, is to foster within each person and in each community an identity that speaks to them of God. As abbot, Hume beseeched newcomers to his Community, saying, 'be yourselves. Understand that the Community accepts you totally and wants you as you are and you must feel always totally acceptable and totally accepted,'[93] and repeated it to the Benedictines gathered at St Vincent's: 'We must be ourselves, combining virtues of humility and modesty with confidence in ourselves.'[94] By focusing on being Benedictine, Hume told his Community, 'Enjoy being a monk. Be proud to be a monk.'[95] On another occasion, a Chapter at renewal of vows, Hume reminded the Community, there should be 'a general enthusiasm for all that we are and all that we do,'[96] put another way, Benedictines should radiate these qualities that draw others to God. In this way Hume understands the mature Benedictine as one whose being flows from charity to charity; whose doing follows as total commitment to the service of God and neighbour. So, with monastic instinct understood as an ever-growing awareness of what is fitting for their vocation and what is not, they are able to live the art of being Benedictine, which can now be more clearly understood as the art of seeking God. For Hume, seeking God's will requires each to be adaptable 'to the will of Almighty God',[97] and have an 'an availability for the direct service of Almighty God in our prayer and availability to our neighbour—to our brethren in the first instance, and then those whom our ministry, whether here in the monastery or outside in parishes, brings us into contact.'[98]

The Art of Treasuring the Silence of the Desert and Thriving in the Market-place

The trained Benedictine will learn the art of treasuring the silence of the desert. This art thrives in the activity of the market-place. Hume described the desert as 'withdrawal from activity and people to meet God',[99] and the market-place as 'involvement in pastoral situations of one kind or another.'[100] These contrasting environments require a balance between silence, prayer, and activity. The Benedictine must learn the art of balance, especially in a community like Ampleforth, engaged in demanding works in parish, school, and study. The desert and the market-place are essential aspects of being Benedictine, as Hume clearly stated: 'The art of being a monk is to know how to be in the desert and how to be in the market-place.'[101] Although tension exists, true success in the market-place is dependent upon cultivating a life of prayer in the desert, as Hume stated: 'pastoral work will be successful in the true and deepest sense only if the monk is a man of prayer.'[102]

Hume knew the inherent dangers of placing too high an emphasis on work, yet he still placed a high value on the variety of works done by the Ampleforth Community. In order to expand how one might approach work, Hume presented a theology of work: 'our work, by its very nature, draws us closer to God and is, for us individually, immensely beneficial.'[103] Taking the concept of work to another level, Hume believed that work is 'participating in the creative act of God.'[104] Participating in the creative work of God was for Hume most evident in the work of education. Hume shared this 'tremendous vision'[105] with the monks: 'The powers that I have, whatever they are, are powers that are sustained by God, and I am acting as a divine instrument in order to fashion what He would have me fashion.'[106] In education, creative teachers guide their students, sharing with them the knowledge of God gained in the contemplative prayer of the desert. Creative teachers are able to convey to others what they have contemplated. For Hume, that was the purpose of pastoral work: '*contemplata aliis tradere*—to hand on to others things which have been contemplated.'[107]

The academic study of Benedictines in formation should prepare them for both prayer and pastoral responsibilities. Too often studies are viewed as mere drudgery and having no purpose. In addition to preparing the Benedictine to be competent and professional, 'to convey their own personal convictions to other people',[108] Hume presented this theology of study at a Simple Profession:

> No study is ever a waste of time ... it is important to recognize that all pursuit of truth is pursuit of God. Because there must always be, behind every science, that basic principle which alone can illuminate and explain the rest. So there is no knowledge which cannot lead and will not lead, in the end, to God. And there is no knowledge that cannot be informed by prayer, no knowledge which cannot be seen as sharing in the mind of God. And so study, even study of things which don't seem to be immediately relevant to God, can and should lead us to prayer. It is important to have those ideals of study, because

otherwise it can often be a drudge from which one can see little escape.[109]

Simone Weil also recognized this relationship between the art of study and the art of prayer. Weil believed 'The key to a Christian conception of studies is the realization that prayer consists of attention,'[110] and 'although people seem to be unaware of it today, the development of the faculty of attention forms the real object and almost the sole interest of studies.'[111] Persevering with studies, no matter the subject or level of difficulty, students, whatever their level of aptitude, increase their attention span so as to be more attentive to God in prayer. This idea is especially important for those who find study difficult. Study prepares one for prayer; prayer leads one to God.

Attentive persons are better able to serve their neighbour, having the ability to listen attentively and respond with compassion. Christians who prepare for pastoral work with study and prayer, should remember that the most important things are not intelligence or knowledge. Hume, at a Simple Profession Chapter, highlighted two important qualities in a priest as a way of encouraging those who find studies difficult: 'In a priest there are two qualities which are important—common-sense and kindness ... If you add to that intelligence, all fine and good. If one is of limited ability, so be it, although it is a difficulty in the monastic life. Do not become discouraged.'[112] For Weil, 'Academic work is one of those fields containing a pearl so precious that it is worthwhile to sell all our possessions, keeping nothing for ourselves, in order to be able to acquire it.'[113] For Hume, the pearl was prayer learned in the desert. The prayer of the desert teaches the monk 'genuine love of God and man ... Learn it there and you will have something to sell in the market-place—the pearl of great price.'[114] The pearl of academic work and the pearl of prayer are gems which will shine in the market-place.

Even if one understands the relationship between the desert and the market-place, one must learn how to balance them. The first lessons in how to achieve this balance are learned in the desert of the novitiate, where times to 'pray, read, and reflect'[115] are in the timetable. At a Clothing Chapter, Hume described the threefold aim of the novice in the desert of a novitiate, when confronted with fears and anxieties, saying, 'First, you have to get to know God and Him whom He has sent: Jesus Christ Our Lord ... Secondly, you have to get know yourself, and there will be little chance of escaping. You have to face up to what you are; and the discovery may be disconcerting, even alarming. Thirdly, you have got to get to know one another.'[116]

The desert poses these challenges to a novice; they must be faced early in monastic life in order to prepare him or her for the activity of the market-place. The challenges are both about learning one's shortcomings, and the shortcomings of others. In the desert, the novice learns 'the art of community life, with patience, tolerance, generosity, and respect.'[117] As Hume told newcomers, 'You would be a curious lot if you did not at some time in the course of the year get on one another's nerves,'[118] while reminding them of the truth, 'if someone else is getting on your nerves, you are almost certainly getting on his.'[119] Tense moments often arise when one is faced with such irritants, yet they must be faced 'in the charity of Christ.'[120] The wisdom gained from 'knowledge of God, yourself, and your neighbour should lead you to a threefold loving: a love of God, of yourself, and of the brethren',[121] all 'tools for good works'[122] of which St Benedict writes in his Rule, and ones which are put to use in the market-place.

So, the relationship between the desert and market-place is strong, as Hume described:

> *We shall never be safe in the market-place unless we are at home in the desert* ... The heart, too, must learn to live in its desert if it is to be capable of involvement in the market-place. It is only in the desert that you can learn to turn loneliness into solitude, and it is only when we have learnt solitude and freedom—the capacity to be alone—that we can be safely involved with others.[123]

He added, 'because we are involved in the market-place it is crucial for us to appreciate the desert. A monk is valuable in the market-place if he preserves a nostalgia for the desert: a nostalgia to be
a man of prayer, leisure for prayer, the desire for prayer—hanging
on to this, never letting go; this it is which fits us for God's call
to be involved with people and activity.'[124] And nostalgia for the
desert comes by embracing silence.

Silence is not just a novitiate discipline; the monastery should
be a place of silence, an environment where all learn to treasure
the art of silence. St Benedict urges, 'Silence should be sought at
all times by monks and nuns, and this is especially important for
them at night time.'[125] All in a monastery have the right to expect
an atmosphere of silence, not only for their own good, but for the
good of others. Hume spoke of silence together with recollection
and prayer as 'the "sine qua non" of living for and with God.'[126]
He added, 'Silence is for recollection and recollection is the first
prerequisite for prayer, it is the prerequisite for adverting to the
presence of God and so of learning to live in the presence of God.
This is the value of silence in the religious life.'[127] Silence is an art
to be learned and treasured.

Practising the art of silence, Benedictines learn to maintain an
awareness of the close presence of God, which should guide all
thoughts and actions. This is especially true during the *Summum
Silentium*, the silence after Compline, when 'no one will be permit-
ted to speak further.'[128] This is the silence which prepares one to
create other silent spaces throughout the day and 'see these places
and times of silence as the very basis of a mature, adult spiritual
life.'[129] The silence after Compline is not a time for visiting, watching television, or working on the computer. It is time to be more
aware of the presence of the Lord and fill ourselves with His love
and mercy. Filled with the Lord, Benedictines grow in charity, in
service of God, and in service of one another.

The tapestry of Benedictine life is held together by the delicate
balance between a life of prayer and a life of action. The silence
of the desert is essential for the cultivation of a life of prayer. The

tendency is to escape from facing the challenges of learning about oneself and others and to seek refuge in the activity of the market-place. To save one from such detriments to spiritual growth, Hume remarked, 'there should be in every monk a potential Trappist, a potential Carthusian',[130] or rather, 'there should be a little regret in each one of us that God did not call us to be a Carthusian: a regret that this great vocation was not offered to us. If we have that thought within us, we will be saved from activism: will be spared the danger of failing to see the hand of God in our lives, the hand of God in our work.'[131] Hence the importance of stepping back, reflecting, and being responsible for and faithful to a life of prayer, learned in the novitiate, practised throughout life. Over time, then, one begins to yearn for the desert where a person is renewed and refreshed. It is in the desert that a person establishes and nurtures a relationship with the Lord, becomes intimate with Him through prayer and silence. The closer one becomes to the Lord, the better able he or she is to love and serve others and therefore thrive in the market-place, ever aware of God's presence.

Hume pointed to St Benedict and St Ignatius as models of the importance of withdrawing before engaging in work: 'Just as St Benedict, and indeed St Ignatius, before they started their life's work went into the cave to be alone with God, so constantly right through life, one has to be going back into the cave to be alone with God. One has to enter, so to speak, into the darkness of one's soul in order to come out into the light of day and see things clearly.'[132] Treasuring the art of the silence of the desert, Benedictines learn the art of thriving in the market-place.

The Arts of Humility and Obedience

Humility and obedience are arts upon which Benedictines base their lives, gifts they cultivate while searching for God. Only the humble and obedient can find the God whom Hume called

elusive: 'God is elusive—sometimes very elusive—and I think
that you will discover that your finding of God will be a spas-
modic thing. There will be moments, and moments early on in
your monastic life, when God seems to be close and then that
will be followed by periods when God seems to be remote.'[133]
Hume added: 'Those periods of remoteness on the part of God
are to draw us into a new kind of search, a new way in our internal life of seeking God. God hides, in order that we should be
more active in our search for Him, in order, often, that we should
acquire something else',[134] that is, humility. Growth in humility
'enables us to understand the majesty and the greatness of God
and the smallness of our own selves.'[135] In order to learn the art
of humility, Benedictines must recognize the need for grace to
help them sustain the search for an elusive God, who often reveals
Himself in unsuspected places and unlikely people. Only the
humble can welcome all as Christ and show proper honour to
all.[136] Hume stated, 'Our discovery of God—I see this more and
more clearly—is in proportion to our growth in humility.'[137] It is
only with humility that Benedictines can respond in obedience.
Recognizing again the need for grace, Hume urged the monks
'to treasure obedience, to value it, to love it. It is gift from God.'[138]

   To see the clear connection between the art of humility and
the art of obedience, one need only compare and contrast St
Benedict's two chapters on obedience with the longest chapter in the Rule, on humility, presented as a ladder—a ladder
which one descends by pride and ascends by humility. 'The first
step of humility', writes St Benedict as he begins chapter 5, 'is
unhesitating obedience'.[139] In chapter 7, St Benedict teaches, 'The
third step of humility is to submit oneself out of love of God
to whatever obedience under a superior may require of us',[140] a
teaching repeated and broadened in chapter 71: 'Obedience is
of such value that it should be shown not only to the superior
but all members of the community should be obedient to each
other'.[141] In these verses, St Benedict echoes St Paul's great hymn
on humility and obedience: Christ, 'though he was in the form of

God, did not regard equality with God something to be grasped, but emptied Himself, taking the form of a slave, being born in human likeness. And being found in human form, He humbled Himself and became obedient to the point of death, even death on a cross' (Ph 2:6–8).

In the tradition of St Paul and St Benedict, Hume placed great emphasis on the two closely related arts of humility and obedience, stressing their importance to newcomers at Clothing Chapters. Monastic life, stated Hume, 'would not be authentic unless it is based on humility and obedience',[142] what he called 'the great monastic virtues'[143] Benedictines should think about, learn about, and 'above all practice.'[144] Monastic life flows from and leads to charity as Hume repeated: 'if the purpose of the monastic life, just as the Christian life, is to love God and love one's neighbour, there will, for a monk, be no true love of God or any true love of the neighbour, unless it is firmly based on humility and obedience.'[145]

The arts of humility and obedience are essential to the search for God. Without embracing both, Benedictines are unable to learn the art of searching for God in the monastic way of life. St Benedict stresses as much in the first verses of the Rule: 'Listen carefully, my son, to the master's instructions, and attend to them with the ear of your heart.'[146] Only the humble and obedient Benedictine can be attentive and look and listen for the voice of God in the silence of the desert, for the voice of God in the abbot, and for the voice of God in the brothers and sisters. Hume called 'listening and looking'[147] an 'attitude'[148] that a Benedictine should have 'throughout his life, if his exploration is to be real and his search effective.'[149] Next, St Benedict addresses his message to those who have 'drifted through the sloth of disobedience'[150] and are now ready to give up their own will 'once and for all, and armed with the strong and noble weapons of obedience to do battle for the true King, Christ the Lord.'[151] Placing such importance on humility and obedience can be rather shocking to the person who enters the portal of the monastery, especially in modern times. Contemporary society reveres people who are not only clever but who confidently tout their accolades, honours, and successes, and listen to and obey no one save themselves. Nevertheless, the Benedictine is confronted with the challenges of humility and obedience from the start and Hume wanted newcomers to be prepared. Echoing St Benedict, Hume affirmed the positive and urged novices to 'take every opportunity to exercise true obedience and every opportunity to grow in humility,'[152] for the more one grows in humility, 'the more one sees the value of obedience.'[153] That said, learning to appreciate the value of humility and obedience is difficult and painful, especially for those who have been living in a culture which places little value on their importance.

Unfortunately, humility and obedience are often associated with weakness of character, limited intelligence and immature behaviour. The true Benedictine sees the humble and obedient as strong in will, liberated in behaviour, and mature in relationships: the humble and obedient recognize their total dependence on God. 'This fundamental, ontological dependence of man on God is the very basis of the religious life.'[154] It frees humanity from the 'self', that is, self-seeking, self-fulfilling, self-expressing, self-promoting, which if nothing else, drain one of energy. Most importantly, self-seeking inhibits the work of grace: 'If we are ultimately seeking ourselves this makes us less receptive of the grace of God.'[155] By embracing humility and obedience and all things which lead to God, the Benedictine puts God at the centre of daily life. While growing in monastic stature, the Benedictine is free to love and to serve God and neighbour. Open to grace, Benedictines 'become powerful instruments for good in the hands of God',[156] they 'recognize that whatever achievements we shall have in our monastic life, will be the work of God, the grace of God, so that with the psalmist we will say, "non nobis Domine, non nobis, sed nomine tuo da gloriam"'.[157]

Humility and obedience are about developing the same mind of Christ Jesus. Just as Hume called looking and listening the attitude of the Benedictine, humility is the 'basic attitude which we have to have before God; and obedience follows from it.'[158] Conforming themselves to Christ, the humble look and listen and are able to respond in obedience to Christ who said, 'I have come not to do my own will, but the will of the one who sent me.'[159] Growing in humility, the Benedictine becomes more willing and available to obey even under the most trying circumstances. For Hume, obedience 'is a sign of my availability, not necessarily in terms only of action, of doing—which the words "sharing" and "giving" connotate—but also in terms of accepting, of being prepared to accept God's will even if it means being passed over, being asked to relinquish some responsibility; or just being forgotten.'[160] For anyone who has experienced such situations, these are often the most painful, those which can shatter a fragile ego. Hume said, 'Curiously, it is often not what you are told to do that hurts, but being removed from things which you like doing.'[161] Such daily frustrations, set-backs, and disappointments, which often reveal human weaknesses, imperfections, and faults can be experienced as humiliating. Signs of despondency and depression in Benedictines, are, for Hume, 'a manifestation of pride; and what a golden opportunity for growth in humility.'[162] All imperfections and weaknesses are part of human nature. The sooner novices learn that they are not perfect, and that no one else is either, the more quickly they will grow in spiritual maturity. Communities are comprised of *saints in the making*, everyone is on a journey to holiness. During this journey, wounds are inflicted and healing is needed. Hence the importance of St Benedict's teaching to never 'turn away when someone needs your love.'[163] Humility, though, is not the same as being humiliated, or experiencing humiliations, but it takes a humble person to accept what Hume preferred to call 'contradictions'.[164] Hume, not surprisingly, assists in learning how to put contradictions into proper perspective:

> Are you prepared to embrace a life in which obedience
> plays an important part; and are you prepared to accept
> humiliations?—the word is *opprobria* in Latin. The

word 'humiliations' is a mistranslation; I take it to mean
contradictions—those things which stand in the way, those
things which put us 'out of sorts', those things which come
to depress, and the rest. There comes a crucial moment in
the life of a novice and a young monk when he ceases to
think of his monastic life as something which is there for
him to attain through self-fulfilment, or realisation, or even
his own personal happiness. He moves from that position
to recognising it as a response to a 'call': a call made in
which he answers: 'Yes, I answer that call'. This involves a
considerable difference of mind.[165]

Humility and obedience include accepting that there are others
whose ideas, opinions, or plans are not only better than our own
but take precedence over our own. Hume believed this is what St
Benedict had in mind when he spoke about mutual obedience; he
did not mean 'being reduced to being mere automata',[166] or just
'taking orders from others; he meant, rather, accepting the limitations which others impose upon us by the very fact that there
are "others".'[167] Connecting obedience with humility, St Benedict
describes such situations in the fourth step of humility, whereby
the Benedictine is obedient 'under difficult, unfavourable, or
even unjust conditions'[168] and not only 'embraces suffering',[169]
but 'endures it without weakening or seeking escape.'[170] One
might simply ask novices if their difficulties or aggravations are
going to ruin their vocations, preventing them from answering
'yes' to the call of God.

The humble and obedient also learn to be *detached*. Hume
related the story of one monk who enthusiastically and wholeheartedly threw himself into whatever task he was given, 'Yet
inwardly he was detached. When asked to relinquish tasks he had
done for a long time he accepted this with extraordinary simplicity and ease.'[171] With such an attitude, 'the true worth of this monk
was revealed: he had accepted under obedience the circumstance
determined by his Superiors, and they had sanctified him.'[172] The
monk had mastered the art of being Benedictine, displaying a

humility which allowed him to recognize that he was not the only one suited for a particular task. Such an extraordinary and rare display of obedience and humility enabled the person to support and encourage the successor assigned to the task, and protected him from murmuring, 'the worst of all monastic faults'.[173]

Hume describes what St Benedict means by murmuring: 'murmuring, grumbling, being always critical—critical of persons, of how things are done, continually voicing your criticisms, being unable to accept decisions, being "put out". That kind of thing is pernicious.'[174] Furthermore, and rather startling, 'murmuring is detrimental to the spiritual life. It betrays non-acceptance of the present situation: and the present situation in which we find ourselves is the one in which God wants us to be.'[175] Such a reality puts matters into perspective and may encourage the murmuring monk to learn the art of speech, re-reading St Benedict's chapter 6, 'Restraint of Speech', where St Benedict reminds his followers, 'In a flood of words you will not avoid sin'.[176] The only acceptable kind of obedience for St Benedict is obedience that is 'not cringing or sluggish or half-hearted, but free from any grumbling or any reaction of unwillingness.'[177] St Benedict continues, echoing St Paul, 'Furthermore, the disciples' obedience must be gladly given, for God loves a cheerful giver.'[178] So, obedience for St Benedict is joyful, given gladly, with a freedom to listen to the abbot, and subsequently to obey what is asked, even if the assignment is difficult. Hume begged the monks not to be grumblers, or murmurers, so important for the overall health of the Community: 'If you want to be humble, free, detached; if you are seeking God, wanting Him alone, then cheerfully (God loves a cheerful giver) and good-naturedly you will be able to achieve good things for and within the Community',[179] for 'The more free you are, the more you will want to obey. That is why, for St Benedict, obedience is linked closely with humility.'[180]

Growth in the spiritual life, then, is not possible without the art of humility and its companion, the art of obedience; being in right relationship with God, with creation, with others, and with self is not possible if one does not adopt the Christ-like attitudes of humility and obedience. Hume said, 'When all is said and done, the difference between a spiritual person and an unspiritual person is the difference between a humble person and a proud person ... humility is the finest and nicest quality in a person and it is the hardest and most difficult to achieve.'[181] The one who embodies humility 'makes for a good and an attractive human being',[182] and it follows that the obedient also makes for a good and attractive human being. The humble and obedient have an accurate sense of self, are able to laugh at themselves and do not take life too seriously. Hume advised monks to keep personal and communal matters in perspective:

> Be cheerful. Do not get upset by small things. And do not ever think that a monk should be serious—well, he must be serious, but must never lose his sense of humour— and if you have not got one, then acquire one. A sense of humour is part of humility. It means you do not take yourself too seriously and that you do not get things that go on in monastic life out of proportion: be able to smile at us and at yourselves. That is most important.[183]

Free from the burden of promoting self, the humble and obedient notice the gifts in others and are able to compliment and encourage, harbouring neither hatred, jealousy, nor envy.[184] When the humble and obedient person notices something good in themselves, they give credit to God, not to themselves.[185] The humble and obedient freely and joyfully use their gifts 'so that in all things God may be glorified.'[186] If those who seek God focused solely on becoming more humble and obedient throughout life, they would find the God they seek. While learning the arts of being humble and obedient, they embrace the *good zeal* of Benedictines,[187] and will be faithful and joyful companions with those who compete 'in obedience to one another'[188] so as to 'quickly arrive at that perfect love which casts out fear.'[189]

The Art of Being a Prayerful Benedictine

When considering the art of prayer for the Benedictine, one must remember the essential elements of prayer as laid out in the Rule of St Benedict, namely: Benedictine prayer is humble, regular, communal and scriptural. First, Benedict stressed the relationship between humility and prayer when speaking about *reverence in prayer*: 'Whenever we want to ask a favour of someone powerful, we do it humbly and respectfully, for fear of presumption. How much more important, then, to lay our petitions before the God of all with the utmost humility and sincere devotion.'[190] Only the Benedictine who has learned the art of humility can learn the art of prayer for '*humility* is the foundation of prayer.'[191] Hume, too, stressed the connection between humility and prayer, encouraging monks to treasure both throughout their monastic lives: 'Dear brothers, just finally may I urge you to do two things: study always to become humble; and secondly, love and value prayer. A monastic life which doesn't cultivate humility and which hasn't got prayer is unreal and is courting disaster.'[192] The disaster is that the Benedictine will forget the purpose of monastic life. By cultivating humility and prayer, Hume told the monks, 'you will come to that love of God, and that true love of your fellow men, which is why you have come to this Community.'[193]

Second, Benedictine prayer is regular and communal. St Benedict devotes some thirteen chapters to the celebration of the Divine Office,[194] what he calls the *Opus Dei*, or *Work of God*. In those chapters, Benedict lays the groundwork for the Work of God which centres on the prophet's call, 'Seven times a day have I praised You.'[195] St Benedict expected his monks to gather at seven specified times during the day, and one additional time during the night.[196] At those times they praised God mainly with psalmody and readings from the Old and New Testaments. St Benedict also accepted the norm that the whole psalter be prayed in one week.[197] St Benedict believed that 'idleness is the enemy of the soul,'[198] and so organized a daily schedule that revolved around the communal celebration of the Divine Office. All other activities in the monastery are extensions of communal prayer, including manual labour, and prayerful reading, called *lectio divina*. Communal prayer is so important for sanctifying the hours of the day in the monastery that St Benedict simply states: 'Nothing is to be preferred to the Work of God.'[199] The Divine Office defines Benedictine life—it is 'the *"source and summit of the monastic day,"* typical element of monastic spirituality and *"spiritual summit"* of the monastic life.'[200] All else flows from the celebration of the Divine Office, as Hume said, 'the service of God springing from prayer, that is our life.'[201]

The many hours of the day spent singing God's praises are meant to keep Benedictines aware of the presence of God in their lives, a reminder of their belief 'that the divine presence is everywhere and that in every place the eyes of the Lord are watching the good and the wicked ... especially true when we celebrate the Divine Office.'[202] Though it is difficult to maintain a 'perpetual awareness'[203] of God, awareness of God must at least grow. Awareness of God is dependent upon the amount of time spent in prayer, as Hume told the monks: 'prayer strengthens and enlivens an awareness which will grow weak in proportion as we do not pray. An awareness of God's presence is the fruit not the cause of prayer.'[204] Hence St Benedict's exhortation to 'devote yourself often to prayer.'[205] God continuously invites humanity to be aware of His presence, to respond to His invitation to develop a relationship with Him in prayer. By praying, then, we 'try to make ourselves aware of God and in that awareness respond to him. It is an attempt to raise our minds and hearts to God.'[206] Hume called prayer the '*unum necessarium*: the highest form of union with God that we can attain in this world. If each one of us strives constantly to be a man of prayer, it follows that he will be a man of God. And if that is so, this house will be what it should be: a house of God.'[207]

Third, Benedictine prayer is scriptural just as Benedictine life is scriptural. Sacred Scripture was the foundation of St Bene-

dict's search for God. Therefore, St Benedict does not hesitate
to announce the importance of Sacred Scripture in the lives of
those who embrace the art of searching for God. With energy,
St Benedict calls:

> Let us get up then, at long last, for the Scriptures rouse us
> when they say: *It is high time for us to arise from sleep* (Rm
> 13:11). Let us open our eyes to the light that comes from
> God, and our ears to the voice from heaven that every
> day calls out this charge: *If you hear His voice today, do not
> harden your hearts* (Ps 94[95]:8).[208]

Benedictines, with the attitude of looking and listening, are called
to be alert and ready, to arise from sleep and lethargy. St Benedict continues, 'Clothed then with faith and the performance of
good works, let us set out on this way, with the Gospel for our
guide, that we may deserve to see Him who has called us to His
Kingdom.'[209]

It was not only the Gospel that St Benedict relied on, for the
Rule is saturated with biblical quotations and allusions to Sacred
Scripture as a whole. The Bible was a major point of reference
for St Benedict. Benedictines turn to the whole of the Scriptures
for instruction, to lead them on the path to God. Everyone in
the monastery must pray for the grace to be transformed by the
Word and to obey the Word with the freedom bestowed on them
as children of God.

Regarding the art of prayer, Hume stated, when praying the
psalms, 'we pray in Christ, and with Christ, and indeed Christ
prays in us to the honour and glory of His Father.'[210] As sharers
in divine nature (see 2 Pt 1:4), humanity prays through Him,
with Him, and in Him. Humanity speaks to Christ, and Christ to
humanity. As sharers in divine nature, Benedictines remember:
'Our monastic life is a search for God; it is through Christ, with
Christ and in Christ that we must look.'[211]

Called to be transformed by the Word in a daily of life of prayer,
Hume taught his monks to be responsible to a 'life of prayer'.[212]

No matter the demands placed on Benedictines, they should never diminish the primacy of prayer in their lives. If prayer is diminished, a 'monastic vocation is defective'.[213] With that sobering thought, Hume allowed no compromises and practised his preaching 'that every superior of a religious community is bound from time to time to talk about prayer.'[214] At the end of the day, each monk, including the abbot, can reflect on Hume's question: 'In seeking God, we need constantly to ask ourselves whether prayer has the place in our lives that it should. Do we really think and act as if prayer came first—before anything else whatever?'[215]

It may be easy to intellectually grasp that prayer takes precedence over all things Benedictine, but learning the art of prayer does not come without its challenges. If nothing else, Hume constantly stressed the difficulties encountered in prayer. Maintaining a sense of humour, Hume stated, 'No one prays easily at first, just as I think no one really enjoys the first glass of beer. You've got to get used to beer, then you get hooked on it and want more and more! Prayer is like that, you have got to get hooked but at the beginning it is hard going.'[216] The key to learning the art of prayer is perseverance. If all else fails, pray for perseverance. Why is the art of prayer difficult? Hume explained, 'It is difficult knowing it must go on year after year, always trying to pray, and to pray better. It is a difficulty one must face squarely and fairly.'[217] The art of prayer is also difficult 'because we remember too infrequently that ultimately prayer is a gift from God, but the gift comes, I am sure it comes but only after solid perseverance.'[218]

Looking through a contemporary lens, St Benedict writes of two kinds of prayer: one public, that is, the Divine Office, which, as stated by the Second Vatican Council, is 'a source of holiness and of nourishment for personal prayer, insofar as it is the public prayer of the Church';[219] the other private or personal prayer, including prayerful reading.[220] St Benedict does not give much instruction on how to pray, other than to pray always. He tells Benedictines that the Lord will listen to their prayers,[221] and that when singing the psalms, their minds should be in harmony with their voices,[222] itself an expression of the community's unity. St Benedict mentions that prayer should be 'short and pure, unless perhaps it is prolonged under the inspiration of divine grace.'[223] Similarly, communal prayer 'should always be brief.'[224] After laying out the distribution of the psalms, St Benedict gives the abbot the flexibility to 'arrange whatever he judges better.'[225] In addition, it is the abbot's responsibility 'to announce, day and night, the hour for the Work of God',[226] unless the task is delegated 'to a responsible member of the Community.'[227]

Hume also does not expound upon the complexities of prayer. He, like St Benedict, offers no systematic treatise on prayer. What is important is St Paul's reminder that 'we do not know how to pray as we ought' (Rm 8:26). By acknowledging our inability to pray, 'we are ready to receive freely the gift of prayer.'[228] The pray-er, then, is encouraged, believing that 'the Spirit will come to the aid of our weakness' (Rm 8:26). Relating to the brethren while keeping things simple and practical, Hume gives suggestions on how to approach prayer and also what to do when one feels unworthy, or finds prayer tiresome, overwhelming, or irrelevant. Recalling 'perhaps the most golden sentence in the whole of the Bible',[229] he used the example of the Pharisees, who 'missed the whole point.'[230] Commenting on the call of St Matthew, 'those who are well do not need a physician, but the sick do' (Mt 9:12), Hume said:

> You, my dear brethren, and I can so easily live through life missing the whole point. You think that because you don't find prayer easy, you think that attendance at Mass is something which is less than congenial, you think that because your record in the service of God is not a good one, then the things of God are not for you. Can't you see that the more inadequate you are, the more you need God's help?[231]

With good reason, then, Hume supports and encourages the monks in their life of prayer. In his teaching, Hume distinguishes between two approaches to prayer, one speaks of an 'attitude',[232] the other of an 'internal attraction'.[233] The *obligation to pray* is more an attitude of 'I ought to pray'.[234] It is true that all monks are obliged to pray, but hopefully fulfilling an obligation will lead to *desire*, or want. What has to grow within each monk is 'a desire for prayer, a nostalgia for prayer, a taste for prayer',[235] which only follows from practice of prayer. As Hume stated, 'It is not because we are drawn to prayer that we first begin to pray; more often we have to begin prayer, and then the taste and the desire for it come.'[236] By beginning to pray, Benedictines collaborate with the work of grace and respond to 'the living and true God' who 'tirelessly calls each person to that mysterious encounter known as prayer.'[237]

Sustained by grace, Benedictines continuously respond to the ever-faithful God's call and pray for the taste and desire to pray, even when they think their prayer life is going well. Circumstances will arise which make prayer difficult or burdensome, such as being preoccupied with many obligations, or suffering from fatigue due to stress or exhaustion. Some might feel that God is not even listening, or speaking! At these times, Hume suggested that one might resort to *vocal prayer*, 'the use of a set formula',[238] or divide the thirty minutes of mental prayer into smaller segments, where one could focus on different aspects of the Mass, for example, the Kyrie, then the Gloria, then reflecting on the Prayer over the Gifts, and then parts of the Eucharistic Prayer.[239] Hume prepared the monks to expect difficult situations: 'There can be no serious practice of prayer which is not accompanied by darkness and a sense of unreality',[240] they are 'part and parcel of prayer.'[241] Moments of darkness and aridity are frustrating, even dangerous. The danger is in stopping prayer. Two qualities of a monk are essential at these times, namely, 'tenacity and perseverance'.[242] Faith is purified at these times of frustration.[243] Believe in the God who has called you out of darkness into His wonderful light (see 1 Pt 2:9), for 'darkness is a joy when it heralds the arrival of the light.'[244]

If Benedictines find the Divine Office difficult or burdensome, or are losing the taste for prayer, they might ask themselves if they are being faithful to *lectio divina*, or spiritual reading. Hume called *lectio divina* 'the necessary pre-requisite for a lively and true prayer; a necessary pre-requisite for concentration on the Divine Office.'[245] Persevering with study also assists in increasing attention span, as mentioned earlier, but *lectio divina* is not study. Hume was clear that *lectio divina* is 'not preparation for a sermon, not reading theology for its own sake,'[246] instead it is 'prayerful reading which enables the Holy Spirit to move our minds towards an understanding of, an insight into, the things of God, coupled with a desire to give ourselves to God and to express this in prayer.'[247] *Lectio divina*, then, is not an intellectual pursuit, rather it is for personal transformation, for growing into the image and likeness of God, for learning more about God so as to serve Him and to love Him. *Lectio divina* is risky and demands courage; we never know what God will ask of us. Again, faith is purified, for we believe and trust that God will lead us on the right path as we seek to understand and do His will. Then we proclaim with St Anselm, 'I believe in order to understand', knowing full well that we will never fully comprehend.

Hume taught the monks that they could prepare for prayer in two practical and sensible ways: *remote preparation* and *immediate preparation*. Both types of preparation are suitable for the Benedictine who has learned to treasure the art of silence. Remote preparation can be done at night during the *Summum Silentium*, when the Benedictine prepares for the next morning's public and private prayer. It is important that private prayer be 'planned, and organized and attacked realistically.'[248] The plan may change, but at least one has prepared in advance. With no plan, the tendency is merely to 'mooch'[249] in the Lord, just looking *at* God, and not looking *for* Him, which for Hume is *contemplation*. Hume explained, 'Contemplation is not just looking at God; for most of us, now *in via*, it consists in looking *for* God'.[250] Emphasizing the work of grace, he added, 'if from time to time some "sight" of

Him is accorded, this will be a glimmer granted by grace in what will always be a "cloud of unknowing"".[251] The Church teaches grace as 'a participation in the life of God. It introduces us into the intimacy of Trinitarian life'.[252] Hume's thoughts on contemplation expand this teaching: 'looking for God is done through, with, and in Christ, in unity with the Holy Spirit so that we can give, within that very life of the Trinity, all honour and glory to God, the Almighty Father'.[253] Put in this way, the Benedictine wants to have a plan and be prepared, giving all energy and attention to the praise of the Holy Trinity. With no plan, the tendency is to sleep right through the thirty minutes of private prayer. In that case, one might examine his or her prayer posture and 'adopt one which does not invite sleep'.[254]

During remote preparation, the Benedictine can also form intentions for family, friends, students, colleagues, or the world. To better prepare for the celebration of the Divine Office, the Benedictine can 'look for friends among the psalms'.[255] Look at the psalms that will be prayed the next morning, or psalms which have been studied, or will be studied. Pick one out and 'mull over it during mental prayer ... make it your friend'.[256] Hume encourages Benedictines to work hard to turn the psalms into prayer, to 'work hard to acquire a love of the psalms.'[257]

One other method of remote preparation is by way of private devotions. 'Choir observance is fostered by private devotions'[258] which 'make the public prayer of the Church a more meaningful experience for oneself.'[259] Hume's idea was that 'you pray the psalms better if you pray the rosary, or other equivalent devotion.'[260] By encouraging the Community to pray the rosary, Hume's teaching was consistent with that of the post-Conciliar Church. In *Sacrosanctum Concilium*, private devotions are encouraged as a means of preparing for and entering the liturgy 'with the dispositions of a suitable heart and mind',[261] while recognizing that all forms of devotions 'in some way derive from [the liturgy], and lead people to it.'[262] The *Directory on Popular Piety and the Liturgy* calls the rosary 'essentially a contemplative prayer, which requires "tranquillity of rhythm or even a mental lingering which encourages the faithful to meditate on the mysteries of the Lord's life.'"[263] After praying the rosary, then, Benedictines can better participate in the Divine Office by entering into it in a more peaceful and prayerful state of heart and mind. While praying the rosary, the Benedictine can meditate on the Paschal Mystery, preparing to enter into the dialogue between the Father and Son in the psalmody. Perhaps most importantly, though, Benedictines can focus on Mary herself who 'heard the word of God and lived by it—she who listened, then pondered in her heart.'[264] Emphasizing the feminine, Hume told the Community, 'It is a feminine trait to listen, to receive, to watch. Perhaps that is why more women pray than men. Perhaps that is why among contemplatives there are more women than men—it is the "feminine" which listens and waits. It is a feminine trait, also, to see, to observe. The wine has run out. Mary notices, and being a woman she has a practical mind.'[265] It is wise for all Benedictines to be mindful of the feminine as exhibited by the Mother of God in the mysteries of the rosary. So doing, the Benedictine remembers to be alert and attentive while listening to the still small voice of the Lord (see 1 K 19:12) in the Psalms. Prepared to do the Lord's will, the Benedictine, with Mary, says, 'May it be done to me according to your word' (Lk 1:38).

Immediate preparation for prayer is as important as a time of silence used for recollection, 'of being conscious of what we are trying to do.'[266] *Statio*, that is, the time for gathering and then waiting in silence before processing into choir, is an ideal time for recollection. Hume explained that the monks prepare for processing 'into the presence of God and it is an external gesture that we need. Surely this is the reason why we wear cowls, in order to remind ourselves that we are engaged in a special duty and therefore we wear a special uniform for it.'[267]

Hume discussed two opposite types of prayer: first, one with which he was not familiar, the *prayer of quiet*, when 'there is an awareness of God in the very depth of our being'.[268] The 'prayer of "incompetence'"[269] by contrast is based on absence of awareness. It can occur both early in monastic life, and later. It is when there is no awareness of God, and therefore no awareness of prayer. The person praying feels abandoned by God, that no progress in the art of prayer is being made. He or she may become depressed. Nothing seems to remedy the situation: vocal prayer, use of the imagination, ideas, words, or images. They become obstacles to prayer, and one wants to stop praying. As painful as the prayer may be, there are great lessons to be learned through the prayer of incompetence. Hume mentioned two: First, learn to be patient and wait, itself a lesson in humility. By waiting, one 'has to grow in humility and in the realisation of the limitations of the human soul',[270] and recognize the necessity of grace. People do not initiate prayer, God does: 'it must be God that gets in touch with us, not *vice versa*.'[271] Second, prayer is about purification of faith. 'It is the naked faith which is a terrifying experience and yet it is the meeting point ultimately between God and ourselves in the depth of our being.'[272] It is through the blind eyes of faith that we encounter the Lord.

As taught by Hume, learning the art of prayer has its challenges. Yet, he reminds Benedictines of two key virtues to face them. 'Fidelity and persistence in the face of all odds, all difficulties, are paramount. These enable us to find again the desire for prayer which, so it seemed, we had lost.'[273] Benedictines must be faithful and pray for the grace to persevere, for prayer is the pearl of great price. Practised in the art of being prayerful, Benedictines grow in awareness of and desire for God. With ever increasing awareness, they gain *insight* into the ways of the Lord so as to love Him and to serve Him and to do His will. The effects of prayer, then, move beyond the individual and beyond the community, affecting the whole Church: 'The success of the life of the Church is in proportion to the fidelity of the priests who preside over her affairs, persevere in their prayers. This is so for the laity also, in their activities as part of the lay apostolate.'[274] Looking further still, 'the world is going to have to learn how to pray'.[275] Through the art of prayer, we raise our minds and hearts to God, who alone can fill the void within.

Reflection

Basil Hume's unique contribution to Benedictine spirituality is one that is creative and enduring. The art of searching for God and the art of charity are seen as overarching arts of this tapestry. Both arts are the *raison d'être* of Benedictine life: 'To seek God; not necessarily to find Him—or not to find Him in the way that you would expect to find Him—but to be seeking Him and seeking Him every day, every year throughout your monastic life';[276] 'this search for God is only our way of expressing our response to His search for us.'[277] The Benedictine seeks God in order to love and to serve Him and to love neighbour and to serve neighbour, which, for Hume, is charity or intimacy with God. These are the reasons for the monastic way of life.

The Benedictine begins to learn the arts within the *narrow*,[278] but necessary environs of the novitiate, where he or she quickly grows in spiritual maturity. The learning, though, goes right through life, in what St Benedict called 'a school for the Lord's service.'[279] The spiritual life of a Benedictine, then, is both an art and a gift, rather than, as the contemporary world might prefer to see it, as a technique or skill. By learning these arts, the Benedictine progresses 'in this way of life and in faith'[280] and slowly develops monastic instinct, whereby he or she knows what is fitting, and what is not. The Benedictine learns the specific art of being Benedictine through the particular arts of silence, work, and study; the community arts of loving, humility, and obedience; the contemplative art of prayer; and the art of peace represented by joy, humour, and enthusiasm. Through these arts, Benedictines learn about the God they seek, and become the men and women whom Hume described as those 'who can talk with conviction, based upon whatever experience God is pleased to give them, about

God Himself, Father, Son, and Holy Spirit, and the love which is the Trinitarian life, finding its correlative in the explanation of the Christian life',[281] so important for the Church now. Benedictines who speak with such conviction are not zealots, but rather those who take 'as axiomatic, that a monk should be pleasing to other people, and pleasant.'[282] These attractive qualities can be found in Benedictines who heed Hume's *fervorino*: 'Don't take yourselves too seriously. Take *life* seriously. Take *God* seriously. But don't, please don't, take yourselves too seriously!'[283]

NOTES

[1] B. Hume, *Searching for God* (New York: Paulist Press, 1978), p. 13.

[2] *Ibid.*

[3] B. Hume, *In Praise of Benedict 480–1980 A.D.* (1981; repr. Petersham, MA: Saint Bede's Publications, 1994), p. 5.

[4] *Ibid.*

[5] B. Hume, unpublished conference, 19 January 1964, used with permission of the Ampleforth Abbey Trust, York.

[6] *Ibid.*

[7] Hume, unpublished conference, 23 October 1973.

[8] *Ibid.*

[9] *Ibid.*

[10] Hume, *Searching for God*, p. 57.

[11] *The Rule of St Benedict*, Prologue 20. Hereafter, *RB*.

[12] *RB* Prologue 49.

[13] Hume, unpublished conference, 17 September 1971.

[14] *RB* Prologue 31.

[15] Hume in J. Mortimer, *In Character: Interviews with Some of the Most Influential and Remarkable Men and Women of Our Time* (New York: Penguin Books, 1984), p. 92.

[16] Hume, *Searching for God*, p. 15.

[17] Hume, unpublished conference, 1966.

[18] Hume, *Searching for God*, pp. 100–1.

[19] Vatican II, Dogmatic Constitution *Lumen Gentium*, 40.

[20] Hume, unpublished conference, 27 November 1963.

[21] Hume, unpublished conference, 10 July 1964.

[22] Hume, unpublished conference, 27 November 1963.

23 Hume, unpublished conference, 19 January 1964.

24 *Ibid.*

25 *Catechism of the Catholic Church* (Libreria Editrice Vaticana: United States Catholic Conference, Inc., 1994), 1827. Hereafter, *CCC*.

26 Hume, *Searching for God*, p. 78.

27 See *RB* 72:5.

28 Hume, *Searching for God*, p. 78.

29 Hume, unpublished conference, 13 September 1964.

30 Hume, *Searching for God*, p. 67.

31 *Ibid.*

32 Hume, unpublished conference, 13 September 1964.

33 Hume, unpublished conference, 17 September 1971.

34 *Ibid.*

35 *Ibid.*

36 Hume, *Searching for God*, p. 28.

37 *Ibid.*

38 *Ibid.*

39 Hume, unpublished conference, 17 September 1971.

40 Hume, unpublished conference, 14 September 1968.

41 Hume, *Searching for God*, p. 86.

42 *Ibid.*, p. 45.

43 Hume, unpublished conference, 4 April 1974.

44 *Ibid.*

45 *RB* Prologue 35.

46 Hume, *Searching for God*, p. 19.

47 *Ibid.*, p. 21.

48 Vatican II, Constitution *Sacrosanctum Concilium*, 116.

49 Hume, *Searching for God*, p. 21.

50 *Ibid.*

51 *Ibid.*

52 *CCC* 2003.

53 *RB* 4:20.

54 *RB* 2:33.

55 *RB* 4:21.

56 Hume, *Searching for God*, pp. 22–3.

57 *Ibid.*, p. 23.

58 *Ibid.*

59 *RB* 58:5.

60 *RB* 58:8.

61 Hume, *Searching for God*, p. 37.

62 *Ibid.*, p. 57.

63 Hume, unpublished conference, 19 January 1975.

64 *Ibid.*

65 See *CCC* 1829.

66 Hume, *Searching for God*, p. 23.

67 Hume, unpublished conference, 18 December 1964.

68 *Ibid.*

69 Hume, *Searching for God*, p. 38.

70 *Ibid.*, p. 175.

71 *RB* 58:7.

72 See *CCC* 2000.

73 *RB* 4:20.

74 Hume, *Searching for God*, p. 38.

75 *Ibid.*, p. 12.

76 *Ibid.*

77 *Ibid.*

78 Hume, *In Praise of Benedict*, p. 29.

79 *Ibid*, p. 30.

80 *Ibid.*, p. 30.

81 *Ibid.*, p. 31.

82 *Ibid.*

83 *RB* 2:16.

84 *RB* 2:34.

85 *RB* 64:19.

86 *RB* 64:17.

87 *RB* 64:19.

88 C. Smith, *The Path to Life: Benedictine Spirituality for Monks and Lay People* (York: Ampleforth Abbey Press, 2004), p. 88.

89 Hume, unpublished conference, 7 September 1968.

90 *RB* Prologue 15.

91 *RB* Prologue 25–7.

92 Hume, *In Praise of Benedict*, p. 44.

93 Hume, unpublished conference, 7 September 1968.

94 Hume, *In Praise of Benedict*, p. 44.

95 Hume, *Searching for God*, p. 87.

96 *Ibid.*, p. 24.

97 Hume, unpublished conference, 4 April 1974.

98 *Ibid.*

99 Hume, *Searching for God*, pp. 32–3.

100 *Ibid.*, p. 33.

101 *Ibid.*

102 *Ibid.*, p. 12.

103 *Ibid.*, p. 94.

104 *Ibid.*, p. 102.

105 *Ibid.*, p. 104.

106 *Ibid.*

107 *Ibid.*, p. 100.

108 Hume, unpublished conference, 22 September 1964.

109 *Ibid.*

110 S. Weil, *Waiting for God*, trans. E. Craufurd (New York: Harper & Row, 1973), p. 105.

111 *Ibid.*

112 Hume, unpublished conference, 22 September 1964.

113 Weil, *Waiting for God*, p. 116.

114 Hume, *Searching for God*, p. 35.

115 *Ibid.*, p. 30.

116 *Ibid.*, pp. 30–1.

117 *Ibid.*, p. 31.

118 *Ibid.*

119 *Ibid.*

120 *Ibid.*

121 *Ibid.*

122 *RB* 4.

123 Hume, *Searching for God*, p. 34.

124 *Ibid.*

125 *RB* 42:1.

126 Hume, unpublished conference, 24 July 1964.

127 Hume, unpublished conference, 23 February 1966.

128 *RB* 42:8.

129 Hume, *Searching for God*, p. 33.

130 *Ibid.*, p. 119.

131 *Ibid.*

132 Hume, unpublished conference, 24 July 1964.

133 Hume, unpublished conference, 7 September 1968.

134 *Ibid.*
135 *Ibid.*
136 See *RB* 53:1–2.
137 Hume, unpublished conference, 7 September 1968.
138 Hume, unpublished conference, 9 October 1967.
139 *RB* 5:1.
140 *RB* 7:34.
141 *RB* 71:1.
142 Hume, unpublished conference, 19 January 1964.
143 *Ibid.*
144 *Ibid.*
145 Hume, unpublished conference, 1966.
146 *RB* Prologue 1.
147 Hume, *Searching for God*, p. 28.
148 *Ibid.*
149 *Ibid.*
150 *RB* Prologue 2
151 *RB* Prologue 3.
152 Hume, unpublished conference, 18 December 1964.
153 Hume, unpublished conference, 7 September 1968.
154 Hume, unpublished conference, 27 November 1963.
155 Hume, unpublished conference, 20 March 1967.
156 *Ibid.*
157 *Ibid.*
158 Hume, unpublished conference, 1966.
159 *RB* 5:13.
160 Hume, *Searching for God*, p. 84.
161 *Ibid.*, p. 66.
162 Hume, unpublished conference, 12 May 1965.
163 *RB* 4:26.
164 Hume, *Searching for God*, p. 56.
165 *Ibid.*, pp. 56–7.
166 Hume, unpublished conference, 13 September 1964.
167 Hume, *Searching for God*, p. 68.
168 *RB* 7:35.
169 *Ibid.*
170 *RB* 7:36.
171 Hume, *Searching for God*, p. 67.

172 *Ibid.*

173 *Ibid.*, p. 32.

174 *Ibid.*

175 Hume, unpublished conference, 20 February 1969.

176 *RB* 6:4.

177 *RB* 5:14.

178 *RB* 5:16.

179 Hume, *Searching for God*, p. 32.

180 *Ibid.*

181 Hume, unpublished conference, 16 March 1968.

182 Hume, *Searching for God*, p. 31.

183 Hume, unpublished conference, 7 September 1968.

184 See *RB* 4:65–7.

185 See *RB* 4:42.

186 *RB* 57:9.

187 See *RB* 72.

188 *RB* 72:6.

189 *RB* 7:67.

190 *RB* 20:1–2.

191 *CCC* 2559.

192 Hume, unpublished conference, 9 October 1967.

193 *Ibid.*

194 See *RB* 8–20.

195 *RB* 16:1.

196 See *RB* 16.

197 See *RB* 18:23–5.

198 *RB* 48:1.

199 *RB* 43:3.

200 A. Field, ed., *The Monastic Hours: Directory for the Celebration of the Work of God and Directive Norms for the Celebration of the Monastic Liturgy of the Hours*, 2nd ed. (Collegeville: Liturgical Press, 2000), p. 16.

201 Hume, unpublished conference, 18 March 1964.

202 *RB* 19:1–2.

203 Hume, *Searching for God*, p. 188.

204 *Ibid.*

205 *RB* 4:56.

206 Hume, *Searching for God*, p. 126.

207 *Ibid.*, p. 76.

[208] *RB* Prologue 8–10.

[209] *RB* Prologue 21.

[210] Hume, unpublished conference, 16 March 1966.

[211] Hume, unpublished conference, 23 October 1973.

[212] Hume, *Searching for God*, p. 126.

[213] *Ibid.*, p. 56.

[214] *Ibid.*, p. 119.

[215] *Ibid.*, p. 81.

[216] B. Hume, *Cardinal Basil Hume: In My Own Words*, ed. T. de Bertodano (London: Hodder & Stoughten, 1999) p. 94.

[217] Hume, unpublished conference, 19 January 1964.

[218] *Ibid.*

[219] *Sacrosanctum Concilium*, 90.

[220] See *RB* 48:1.

[221] See *RB* Prologue 18.

[222] See *RB* 19:7.

[223] *RB* 20:4.

[224] *RB* 20:5.

[225] *RB* 18:22.

[226] *RB* 47:1.

[227] *Ibid.*

[228] *CCC* 2559.

[229] Hume, unpublished conference, 21 February 1964.

[230] *Ibid.*

[231] *Ibid.*

[232] Hume, *Searching for God*, p. 117.

[233] *Ibid.*

[234] *Ibid.*

[235] *Ibid.*

[236] *Ibid.*, pp. 117–18.

[237] *CCC* 2567.

[238] Hume, *Searching for God*, p. 121.

[239] *Ibid.*

[240] Hume, *Searching for God*, p. 118.

[241] *Ibid.*

[242] *Ibid.*

[243] *Ibid.*

[244] Hume, *In Praise of Benedict*, pp. 37–8.

245 Hume, *Searching for God*, p. 118.

246 *Ibid.*

247 *Ibid.*

248 Hume, unpublished conference, 24 March 1964.

249 *Ibid.*

250 Hume, *Searching for God*, p. 100.

251 *Ibid.*

252 *CCC* 1997.

253 Hume, *Searching for God*, p. 101.

254 Hume, unpublished conference, 24 March 1964.

255 Hume, unpublished conference, 16 March 1966.

256 *Ibid.*

257 Hume, *Searching for God*, p. 51.

258 Hume, unpublished conference, 16 March 1966.

259 *Ibid.*

260 *Ibid.*

261 *Sacrosanctum Concilium*, 11.

262 *Ibid.*, 13.

263 Congregation for Divine Worship and the Discipline of the Sacraments, *Directory on Popular Piety and the Liturgy: Principles and Guidelines* (Boston, MA: Pauline Books & Media, 2002), 197, p. 141.

264 Hume, *Searching for God*, p. 160.

265 *Ibid.*

266 Hume, unpublished conference, 16 March 1966.

267 *Ibid.*

268 Hume, *Searching for God*, p. 123.

269 *Ibid.*

270 *Ibid.*, p. 122.

271 *Ibid.*

272 *Ibid.*

273 *Ibid.*, p. 67.

274 Hume, unpublished conference, 29 November 1967.

275 Hume, *Searching for God*, p. 101.

276 Hume, unpublished conference, 7 September 1968.

277 Hume, unpublished conference, 17 September 1971.

278 See *RB* Prologue 48.

279 *RB* Prologue 45.

280 *RB* Prologue 49.

[281] Hume, *Searching for God*, p. 25.
[282] *Ibid.*, p. 58.
[283] *Ibid.*, p. 27.

Chapter 3

Hume the Pastor

ASIL HUME'S SERVICE AS PASTOR to the people of England
and Wales was rooted in his monastic spirituality. The core
of his message is the relationship between the search for
God and prayer, well stated by Hume: 'We talk of knowing *about*
God, whereas the point is to know God. We want to know God,
that is why there is prayer in our lives. It is only in the experience
of praying that we become aware not only that we seek God, but
that God is always seeking us.'[1] Another theme of Hume's is that
of the spiritual pilgrimage, one touched upon in his service as
abbot but more fully emphasized in his work as Cardinal. For
Hume, 'Life is a pilgrimage. We are on the march, and sooner
or later we shall reach our destination. That destination we call
heaven.'[2] Hume finds 'this pilgrim way not at all easy ... it can be
pretty rough and an uphill business as I try to make my way along
it.'[3] The pilgrim is one who 'wanders through life, often limping,
sometimes bewildered, at times quite lost; and the pilgrim is
searching, often quite unconsciously, for something or someone
to make sense of life, and certainly to make sense of death.'[4]

Reflecting on his life as bishop in *Footprints of the Northern
Saints* while emphasizing his monastic heritage, Hume turned to
two monk saints in particular for inspiration: St Aidan, whom he
called 'the perfect pastor',[5] and St Cuthbert, with whom he shared
'a real love of the monastic life.'[6] About Aidan and Cuthbert,
Hume wrote, 'They remind me that, unless prayer is central in
my life, then I cannot do my job as a bishop as efficiently and cor-
rectly as it should be done.'[7] He continued, 'What I have learned

from Aidan and Cuthbert is the importance of withdrawing from activity from time to time to be alone with God',[8] a lesson which led him to state definitively: 'Unless one can take time to be alone with God, then one is not really thinking pastorally.'[9] That was not all he learned from them though, as he stated, 'I have learned from other people, and from bishops like Aidan and Cuthbert, that I, too, have to be a shepherd. I, too, have to be at the service of other people, especially those most in need.'[10] For Hume, 'Aidan, in particular, was somebody who tried to bring the flock together as a shepherd should, giving them guidance, taking them to pastures where they might feed on the Word of God and on the sacraments.'[11]

There are three statements which reveal Hume's brilliance as pastor, that is, his knack of relating to the ordinary believer who struggles with a life of faith, prayer, and growth in relationship with God. In the first statement, found in the popular *To Be a Pilgrim: A Spiritual Notebook*, Hume places himself at the same level of those whom he led in his work as pastor. He writes: 'These thoughts are being published as one way of fulfilling the role of bishop as teacher ... This book is incomplete and not too systematic—just the thoughts of one pilgrim to help some of the others.'[12] Realizing that he was on the pilgrim journey like everyone else was a lesson in humility he learned in his years as schoolmaster. Hume once remarked:

> As a schoolmaster I learned a very important truth. Looking after boys which was my task, I discovered that every boy between the ages of thirteen and eighteen (which was the age range in which I operated) was in some manner superior to me. He was something I could not be or he could do something which I couldn't do—even if it was only fixing a television set.[13]

The next two statements are taken from his reflections on the priesthood and reveal his gift as communicator of the spiritual life, a unique gift which enabled him to translate the message he gave to his monks into a language understood in the wider Church and beyond. Like his beloved English saints of Northumbria, who 'Because of their own personal transformations into men and women of prayer, God could use them to bring the good news into the lives and hearts of the people to whom they preached',[14] Hume spoke in simple and direct ways about the God he loved which enabled him to touch the lives and hearts of those who heard his message. What he found attractive about the English saints, namely, 'the simplicity of their message and the radical way in which they lived out their own Christian lives',[15] Hume sought to imitate. In the Introduction to his reflections on the priesthood, Hume wrote: 'I have tried in the following pages to retain the simplicity and directness of the spoken word. And they are the words of a pastor and not of a specialist theologian.'[16] Later in the same book Hume told his priests, 'I think there is a great need to find a way of speaking about God which touches the lives and hearts of our people, because there is a search going on. We have so many riches in our tradition from our collective experience; we have simply got to find a way to communicate.'[17]

Although already quoted in Chapter 2, what Hume told John Mortimer bears repeating: 'it's remarkable how many people you can help by saying something quite simple.'[18] Hume's gift of simplicity touched the lives of diverse people, both before and during his time as Archbishop. His confrère Adrian Convery noted: 'I think one the most valuable things about Basil, one of the obvious things, was that he had a tremendous gift for saying very profound things in an extremely simple way. So, when he preached, he was tremendously effective. You always understood what he meant, it wasn't undecipherable or too dense or anything like that.'[19] Another person who made a similar comment was the mother of Princess Diana. Concerning the homily preached by Hume at the Requiem Mass (5 December 1997) for her daughter, the Princess of Wales, she remarked: 'On this occasion, his words were spoken with eloquence and dignity, while at the same time retaining a luminous simplicity of expression which I found boldly directional, captivating and comforting.'[20] She added, 'It is my hopeful prayer that I shall ever remember that sermon.'[21]

Pastor of Prayer

Just as Hume stressed the primacy of prayer in the life of the Ampleforth Community, he did the same in his service as pastor to the people of England and Wales. Choosing not to pray has serious consequences as Hume told priests: 'The failure to develop the practice of prayer in parishes today is responsible for serious spiritual malnutrition.'[22] Alerting priests to their responsibilities Hume said, 'One of the most important pastoral priorities today is to encourage people to pray. Quite apart from the need to learn about prayer, we need it ourselves because without prayer faith becomes dull.'[23] Hume warned priests: 'Without prayer we begin to adopt the values of the world and the danger is that we become that little bit more materialistic, secular, worldly.'[24] All priests should ask themselves, '"Do I pray?" and answer very honestly. And when did we last preach a homily explaining to people how to pray? When did we last preach a homily telling them what prayer is? When did we last sit with a young person and ask: "Have you tried prayer?"'[25]

Prayer, Hume insists, is not reserved for a privileged few: 'the basic principles of prayer are the same for the contemplative nun as they are for the busy housewife. The former has more time and a structured life which makes the opportunities for prayer easier. But it would be a grave mistake to hold that prayer is only for certain people and not for others.'[26] With regard to religious and the life of prayer, Hume stated: 'Every religious engaged in active work should carry within her a disappointment that she is not enclosed in a life of constant, unremitting prayer. In every Sacred Heart nun there should be a disappointed Carmelite; just as in every Benedictine there should be a disappointed Carthusian',[27] something he also told his monks in 1967. What applies to monks applies to all religious: 'Religious should never lose a certain nostalgia for the desert. If they have nostalgia for the desert, then they will be safe in the market place.'[28] But Hume was all too aware of the real situation: 'The ideal would be if all priests and religious were people of prayer but sadly this is not always the case.'[29] In summary, whatever one's state of life, 'We all need to pray. Prayer is to the life of the spirit what breathing is to the life of the body.'[30]

In his interview with John Mortimer, Hume divulged his own struggle with prayer. In response to Mortimer's question, 'What do you feel, when you pray?',[31] Hume replied, 'Oh, I just keep plugging away. At its best it's like being in a dark room with someone you love. You can't see them; but you know they're there.'[32] Hume echoed his sentiments in *Basil in Blunderland* where he spoke of the difficulty he had in trying to communicate with his 'Auntie B—who was very old and extremely deaf.'[33] 'She could not hear what I was saying … disliked telephones anyway'[34] and, he noted further, 'had very little to say.'[35] This experience with his aunt was not unlike his experience of prayer: 'telephoning somebody who appears to be deaf and apparently has nothing to say to us.'[36] With a touch of humour Hume added, 'Sometimes I say to myself that God is like Auntie B, bad on the telephone.'[37]

The humour, the humility, and the vulnerability manifest in this statement are some of the qualities in Hume as pastor which most endeared him to his flock. Cardinal Cahal B. Daly observed: 'The very admission of his failures in prayer, the very simplicity and honesty with which he has written and spoken of his struggles have made Cardinal Hume a great teacher of prayer for the rest of us.'[38] Archbishop Arthur Roche recalled 'an informal gathering of bishops who were talking about prayer,'[39] where Hume was asked 'how he as a former monk and now a bishop prayed. After a momentary awkwardness and a turning in his chair, came the reply, "Oh, I'm such a flop".'[40] Even so, Roche noted,

The personal dedication of Cardinal Basil Hume to prayer
was obvious to anyone who ever knew or met him. He
carried about within himself a still centre that was almost
tangible. It was, I think, the thing that most attracted people
to him. Indeed, it was the source that most informed his
character and gave him that wonderful simplicity and
incisiveness when faced with matters of Church or State.[41]

For Hume, 'The spiritual life and prayer are almost interchange-
able words. There is no serious spiritual life without prayer.'[42]
On spirituality in general Hume commented: 'Entering into the
world of God is one way of describing spirituality. Spirituality is
the soul of religion, its inner dynamism, from which every other
Christian action derives is motivation and its energy. Without it
religion is empty.'[43] Therefore, without prayer religion is empty.
As he did with his monks, Hume continually used what he considered 'the best of all definitions of prayer',[44] namely, the one
from the *Catechism*: 'Prayer is the raising of one's mind and heart
to God.'[45] He felt, however, that 'one word was omitted: trying.
Prayer is *trying* to raise our minds and hearts to God.'[46] And he
went on to say:

> The only 'failure' in prayer is when we neglect it. The only
> 'success' in prayer is the sense of God's presence, or a deep
> peace and sense of well-being, a marvellous moment of
> inner freedom. When that comes, it is a special gift from
> God. We have no claim on it; we cannot demand it. Our
> part is to turn to Him as best we can, trying to raise our
> minds and hearts to Him.[47]

Not limiting himself to only one definition of prayer, Hume also
likened prayer to friendship. He noted: 'Friendships need space
to develop and grow strong. Friends must waste time together. It
is also thus in prayer. Prayer is making friends with God, and He
with us. Prayer is trying to focus the mind on God, and to admit
Him into our hearts. Prayer is wasting time with God. Prayer
needs space to develop and grow strong.'[48] Basically, 'God must

never be a stranger.'[49] Being in relationship with the Lord goes beyond mere friendship, as Hume beautifully expressed:

> Always think of God as your lover. Therefore He wants to be with you, just as a lover wants to be with the beloved. He wants your attention, as every lover wants the attention of the beloved. He wants to listen to you, as every lover wants to hear the voice of the beloved. If you turn to me and ask, 'Are you in love with God?' I would pause, hesitate and say, 'I am not certain. But of one thing I *am* certain—that He is in love with me.'[50]

In order to give our attention to God, and let Him be attentive to us in love, the pray-er needs silence, the art of which Hume learned and taught in the monastery and continued to stress as pastor. Here, Hume highlights Christ's need for silence and ours as well:

> There is one aspect of Christ's life which needs to be constantly underlined and emphasised. From time to time He would withdraw from the crowds and His ministry to be alone with His Father. In that way He showed us the importance of *our* being alone with the Father.
>
> Silence and solitude were part of the life of Our Blessed Lord. In His public ministry, intensely busy, He went off to look for solitude, silence and stillness.
>
> We should do the same from time to time, just to think about the love God has for us. Go back to that constantly.[51]

Moreover, there is another reason for silence, one especially relevant in a present age bombarded with noise and stimulation: 'To be silent and still is an art to be learned. It has its own discipline and difficulties, but the learning of it is essential, lest we be trapped in the purely secular and the material, escaping from the emptiness of the former by indulging in the attractions of the latter.'[52]

Even if one yearns to pray and understands its importance, many may wonder where to begin with prayer, or how to go about it in the midst of a hectic schedule with myriad responsibilities and stresses. Hume provides practical tips or *Ten golden rules* for prayer:[53]

1.   Plan to pray; do not leave it to chance. Select a time and a place (a room at home, on the bus, taking a walk).
2.   Decide on how long you will spend in trying to pray (five minutes, ten, fifteen, thirty or more).
3.   Decide what you are going to do when you pray—e.g. which prayer to select to say slowly and lovingly; or which passage from the Bible to read prayerfully. Sometimes use your own words; sometimes just be still and silent. Follow your inclination.
4.   Always start by asking the Holy Spirit for help in your prayers. Pray: 'Come Holy Spirit, teach me to pray; help me do it'.
5.   Remember you are trying to get in touch with a Person, and that Person is God—Father or Son or Holy Spirit. He is wanting to get in touch with you.
6.   Don't be a slave to one way of praying. Choose the one that you find easiest, and try some other method when the one you are using becomes a burden or doesn't help.
7.   Don't look for results.
8.   If you have distractions, then turn your distractions into your prayer. (If a car passes the window in the wrong gear, then say something to God about the driver—I mean a kind of prayer for the welfare of the driver, not necessarily for his driving or gear box!)
9.   If you always feel dry or uninterested at prayer, then read a spiritual book or pamphlet. An article in a Catholic paper may be a help. Spiritual reading is important.
10. Trying to pray *is* praying. Never give up trying.

As he did with his monks, Hume spoke on many occasions about different types of prayer. In *Basil in Blunderland,* he focuses especially on 'mental prayer' or 'meditation.'[54] In the book, we see Hume on holiday in Scotland, playing hide-and-seek with two 'junior members of the family'[55] he was visiting. At the same time, we see him devoting at least 30 minutes a day to mental prayer. It is in the various hiding places throughout the house that Hume is able to meditate, or try to raise his heart and mind to God. On mental prayer, Hume said, 'It is different from reciting prayers out of a book or from memory, such as morning or night prayers,'[56] although 'These, incidentally, are also quite essential.'[57] Returning to his favourite definition of prayer, he added, 'I have in mind time spent alone with God, trying to raise mind and heart up to Him.'[58] In order to give people direction for their mental prayer or meditation, Hume offered five starting points.

Mental Prayer: First Starting Point

Hume turned to a passage in St Paul's Letter to the Romans: 'For what can be known about God is evident to them, because God made it evident to them. Ever since the creation of the world, His invisible attributes of eternal power and divinity have been able to be understood and perceived in what He has made' (Rm 1:19–20). From this passage Hume understood 'that there are many hints in the created universe of what God may be like. Such hints are no doubt very different from the reality, but nonetheless are helpful.'[59] In other words, looking to the beauty in creation can be a means of raising our minds and hearts to God.

By way of example, Hume spoke on seeing God in those we encounter. As he put it, 'we have been told that we are made in the image and likeness of God. It means that what we see in others may give us some idea of what God is like.'[60] Furthermore, 'If every single person is made to the image and likeness of God, then every single person can tell me something about God which nobody else can,'[61] which may be a rather shocking statement.

It is worthwhile now to look at a conference Hume delivered to the Community at Ampleforth in 1973 in which he addressed personal relationships. What he said then sheds light on the pres-

ent topic of seeing God in others and how one is called to do so
with respect and honour. In the conference Hume expounds
upon the Book of Genesis where we are reminded that 'each
person is in some way an incarnation of God.'[62] Hence, 'Every
human being expresses, or reflects, something of God. Because
each person is unique and different, what each person has to say
about God is unique and different. It may be the character of a
person, or his talents or gifts, or some other quality which will
in some way express to us, if we have eyes to see, the divine.'[63]
Hume continued, 'In no area of human personality is this more
true than in the lovableness of a person. When we discover what
is lovable in a person we can see there reflected and mirrored
the lovableness of God Himself.'[64] There is beauty in the depths
of every person, even in the stranger and in those we might not
find attractive or likeable. As Hume said, 'there is in everybody
something lovable which it is incumbent upon us to discover,
and in the discovery of it we see more clearly in that person one
made to the image and likeness of his or her Maker.'[65]

Accordingly, 'beauty in people, goodness, and nobility may
lead us—should lead us—to think of God.'[66] Hume asked, 'You
see a beautiful person? How much more beautiful is God. Beauty
in Him may well be different, and indeed it is. But a beautiful person or object points to a similar value in Him. God is responsible
for all beauty.'[67] Alluding to Thomas Aquinas, Hume added, 'The
work of art tells us something about the artist.'[68] The same logic
holds for truth and goodness. Hume elaborated: 'You seek truth?
As you do so, you are exploring the mind of God, seeing persons
and things as He sees them. You are drawn to what is good, and
therefore lovable? Then in some manner you are drawn to Him
who is the cause of the good in persons and things.'[69] Hume
clearly explained his point in another publication:

> Some people say that in the artist's work you will see
> something of the artist, and for me this is the nearest
> and best analogy. If you look at a work of art you will

always see something of the artist. Some people can recognise composers: that is Mozart, for example, or that is Beethoven. We leave part of ourselves in what we create, and this is a simple thought about God: He has left part of Himself in His creation. It is through *that* that we can build up our picture of what God is like.[70]

Mental Prayer: Second Starting Point

Hume turns again to Sacred Scripture, this time to the Gospel of St John and what he later called 'a pivotal text for our exploration for what God is like.'[71] Hume first invites the pray-er 'to think about Jesus Christ and listen to His words.'[72] Next, recall 'how one day the apostle Philip said to Jesus: "Show us the Father and we shall be satisfied" (Jn 14:8). Jesus answered: "Philip, you have been with me all this time, have you not realized that he who sees me sees the Father?" (Jn 14:9).'[73] Using 'other words',[74] Hume explains: 'In Our Lord's words, actions, and attitudes we learn in a human way truths about God Himself. Jesus Christ is both God and man.'[75] Hume provides the following example: 'Some words of Our Lord, recorded by St Matthew, can be very consoling to those who, for one reason or another, are in difficulties or in pain. "Come to me, all who labour and are heavy laden, and I will give you rest" (Mt 11:28).'[76] Hume adds, 'These words, like all Christ's words, are personal to each of us, and always relevant. The cultural context may be different, but the truths taught are contemporary in every age.'[77] Hume suggests: 'Read such words as if Our Lord Himself were whispering them into your ear. In fact, He is doing so.'[78] Therefore, one might 'ruminate'[79] on the Lord's words and 'if God so wills it'[80] the words may 'begin to warm your heart. When such words affect you, giving light to the mind and warmth to the heart, it is because the Holy Spirit is at work within you.'[81]

Mental Prayer: Third Starting Point

The third starting point is an extension of the second. Here, Hume suggests repeating 'slowly and, of course, prayerfully a phrase from the Gospel.'[82] For example, 'O God, be merciful to me a sinner' (Lk 18:13), a phrase Hume commented on in another publication: 'I cannot think of any prayer which we can so easily make our own. However burdened we may be by our past sins, or by our present difficulties, however much we may feel ourselves to be failures, and failures in God's eyes, we can always pray: "God, be merciful to me a sinner".'[83]

One might also address the Lord and exclaim, '"Lord, Thou knowest all things, Thou knowest that I love Thee," or "Lord, I believe, help Thou my unbelief" or "Into Thy hands, Lord, I commend my spirit."'[84] Hume calls this last phrase, 'a powerful prayer. They are the words prayed by Our Lord on the Cross.'[85] Hume adds, 'They express, or try to, our total abandonment to God's will.'[86] Hume reminds us that our 'thoughts should be directed to the person you are addressing. The words lead you to think about a person. Our Lord. Then these words may become secondary, and you know—perhaps only in a confused way—that He is present with you.'[87] Thinking about the Lord's presence may be especially helpful for those Hume describes in *The Mystery of Love*, those 'brought up with a wrong concept of God,'[88] whose 'reaction to Him is one of fear or apprehension,'[89] a barrier that 'can take many years to break down.'[90] Hume recommends reflecting on God's love:

> The simple thought that God loves me, and the words used to describe human love such as warmth, intensity, strong, unreserved, all have a meaning in describing God's love. It is quite literally true that no one can, or will ever, love me more than God does; nor will any experience of mine ever, even in the dimmest way, reflect God's love for me. There are no limits to God.[91]

It may also be helpful to meditate on the image of fire as Hume did while taking a rest from the strenuous game of hide-and-seek. Sitting in front of the fire stimulated Hume's thinking: 'A warm and friendly fire is an image of God. Anyway it makes me think of God. The fire is not only friendly, but it is also very active. It is a good image of God, who is quite still, but immensely active.'[92] One might recall the warmth of a friendly fire when choosing to 'walk away from the love which we know God has for us. That is like walking into the cold—and may, also, be going out into darkness, unless the landing light is on. Cold and darkness are symbols of the absence of God. It is sad, and rather frightening, when people are happy to be out in the cold and live in the darkness without God.'[93] Hume offers one final thought: 'Anyone who has wandered away from God should think of coming back into the warmth, that is into the love He offers. There is warmth awaiting us all.'[94]

Mental Prayer: Fourth Starting Point

Another starting point 'is to recite silently and very slowly, a well-known prayer like the Our Father or one of the 150 psalms.'[95] As Hume suggested to his monks, one should make friends with the psalms. 'The psalms',[96] Hume said, 'are particularly wonderful prayers. Our Lord prayed them in His lifetime; the Church, the Body of Christ does so all over the world and in every age.'[97] Appreciating the relationship between Christianity and Judaism, Hume continued, 'The Jewish community prays the psalms. When we do so we are linked to our Jewish roots, and very much in communion with the whole Judaic tradition.'[98] Hume recommends that when reading or reciting the psalms, 'try to go beyond the words to the thoughts they are expressing, and then direct the thoughts to the Person you are seeking to address. There may come a moment when you do not wish to continue reading. You may just want to dwell and rest on a word or phrase that speaks powerfully to you at that moment.'[99] A possible result, adds Hume, is, 'Maybe you will sense the presence of Him whom your heart is seeking. I say maybe, for I do not know whether this can happen often or very rarely.'[100]

Mental Prayer: Fifth Starting Point

Lastly, Hume returned to the *prayer of incompetence*. The *prayer of incompetence* is when the pray-er feels no awareness of God. In *Basil in Blunderland*, Hume associates the prayer to times when 'our minds are possessed by a great worry or agony. We cannot, try as we will, escape from it. It is there, and there it remains.'[101] Or perhaps one is mourning the death of a friend or loved one where 'the sense of grief and sorrow drives out every other thought',[102] times when 'The loss just hurts. Then there will be occasions when physical pain clouds the mind. It seems to mock at fine thoughts.'[103] Hume suggests, 'The way to pray this "prayer of incompetence" is just to be in the presence of God, though this presence will be far from apparent. Just "be" with the pain, and perhaps murmur, "Lord, let this chalice depart from me … but not my will but Thine be done."'[104] On another occasion, Hume called this prayer, the 'prayer of agony',[105] which he also associates to times of 'terrible depression, or some other affliction that keeps us awake at night and anguished all day.'[106]

Reinforcing the value of silence, Hume noted, 'Each of these starting points may well lead to silence. Just to be silent with an awareness of God is a high point of the prayer I have been describing.'[107] Nevertheless, 'For many of us, we get no further than the starting points. The golden moment of silence eludes us.'[108] Never forgetting the necessity of grace, Hume added, 'If the golden moment occurs, it is His gift. If it does not, your prayer is still most pleasing to God. In fact, the starting point may be a point of arrival. A lifetime of starting once again every day makes us different, more Christ-like. Others notice. We don't.'[109] Still, as Hume stated elsewhere, 'We can easily become discouraged if, having made every effort to be persons of prayer, we feel that we are getting nowhere. Perhaps we expect too much to enjoy a sense of God's presence and to delight in it. When it is not thus, we feel that we have failed. It is not so. Our part is to try. God's consolations are His gift.'[110]

There are many lessons to learn from Hume's game of hide-and-seek as related in *Basil in Blunderland*, what one might call insights into the things of God 'prompted by the hiding place.'[111] One in particular stands out as germane to contemporary culture, a culture whose peoples have little time for developing face-to-face personal relationships with others, let alone time to develop and nurture a relationship with God through prayer. When one of the younger players in hide-and-seek hid behind the grandfather clock Hume was impelled to think about time and 'the sacrament of the present moment'.[112] Hume defines *sacrament* as 'an event where God enters into our lives ... an event where Christ meets us and we meet Him.'[113] Not only does Christ meet 'us in the sacraments, especially in the Eucharist',[114] but Christ meets us in the present moment also, the only moment we have. Hume elaborated: 'When you come to think of it the present moment can be a meeting point between God and us. It is only "now," in the present moment, that we meet Him, here and now. Some people spend a lot of time looking back on their lives, others spend time daydreaming about the future, but the important moment is "now."'[115] Hume continued: 'In any present moment we can meet God. At any moment we can just think about God and send a quick message up to Him ... The present moment is always precious. Like a sacrament it is a meeting point between God and ourselves.'[116]

Seeing with the Eyes of Christ

As a pastor *of* prayer, Hume was a pastor *at* prayer, someone engaged with the world, first and last, as a contemplative. Far from ignoring the realities of suffering, hunger, poverty, injustice, and violence, his contemplative approach helped him to be more attentive to these realities and enabled him never to lose sight of the dignity of the human person, no matter how sad or tragic the immediate context. The definition of contemplation he offered the Ampleforth Community is telling: 'Contemplation is not just looking at God; for most of us, now *in via*, it consists in looking *for* God'.[117] Hume looked *for* God in events and in people and not from a distance. This contemplative quality in Hume is an extension of his first starting point for prayer, that is, *seeing* with the eyes of Christ. Hume was in love with God, and as he stated, 'God is lovable, the most lovable of all. A person in love is well placed at that moment to glimpse the meaning of the word "love" as used by God'.[118]

Seeing with the eyes of Christ, Hume looked for God in the eyes, face, touch, and presence of the other. Seeing God in others gave Hume a window into the depth and dignity of the other, and therefore a window into the God of love. Hume once advised, 'Try to see Christ in everyone you meet, and especially in the poor, the sick and the handicapped. Behave towards others as you expect them to behave towards you.'[119] Hume acknowledged his words as 'ancient advice, but very contemporary too.'[120] Hume urged others, 'We can no longer remain indifferent when those who are one with us in Jesus Christ suffer injustice, exploitation and discrimination. We are called to act and to suffer, if necessary, on their behalf.'[121] One of Hume's great pastoral gifts was his ability to *see* with the eyes of Christ enabling him to be truly present with the other and relate to him or her on a deep and lasting level. His presence had a profound effect on others, often amidst tragedy and sadness. Frances Lawrence describes her first meeting with Hume just twelve hours after her husband had been murdered. As she related, 'I cannot remember his exact words on that morning of shadows, only that his pain at man's wanton brutality was tangible. For my children and myself, his presence bestowed an indefinable quietude upon the public noise.'[122] Here one can turn to Pope Benedict XVI: 'Seeing with the eyes of Christ, I can give to others much more than their outward necessities; I can give them the look of love which they crave.'[123]

Hume, by seeing with the eyes of Christ, expressed his love for others by his availability. His being available was especially noteworthy in regard to the priests in his diocese. Hume gave high priority to caring for his priests as he said: 'I think one of my chief anxieties is the welfare and happiness of priests, and I believe that my first responsibility is to look after, to care for priests. How difficult it is to keep in touch with them and to make oneself available to them.'[124] To assist in the caring of priests, Hume had one Vicar General 'specifically appointed to look after the interests of all the active priests of the diocese; another priest is responsible for seeing to the needs of all the retired clergy.'[125] Even so, Hume made efforts to make himself not only personally available but also accessible. Bishop Victor Guazzelli relates, 'Every priest has his private telephone number and is assured of immediate access without having to use an intermediary.'[126] William Charles mentions an occasion when the phone number became a lifeline:

> When one priest in the diocese committed suicide, the young curate in the parish rang the Cardinal's phone number. The Cardinal went to the parish immediately on hearing the news. His concern was not only for the deceased but also for the impact such a tragic event might have on the newly-ordained priest. He spent some time with the young priest and at the weekend it was the Cardinal himself who in effect acted as the 'supply priest', celebrating Masses in the parish and providing a listening ear and a pastoral heart as news of the tragedy spread. As one priest reportedly remarked, for the parishioners and neighbours, 'the Cardinal was Christ walking beside them.'[127]

Seeing with the eyes of Christ, Hume established relationships and opened up lines of communication with priests as Guazzelli notes, 'On many occasions he calls together groups of priests (usually by years of ordination) to spend an evening at Archbishop's House—having a meal together and a few hours of companionship. The priests of the diocese know the Cardinal and Area Bishops better than the priests of thirty years ago.'[128] The result was 'an easiness has come about between the Cardinal, bishops and priests that makes freedom and honesty of speech the norm.'[129] Hume also showed his care and love by seeing Christ in the sick priests or 'those troubled in any way'.[130] Guazzelli adds, 'However heavy his programme may be, he is often the first to visit a sick priest in hospital. It speaks volumes about personal relationships when (as Area Bishops have noted) the first person a troubled priest will turn to is often the Cardinal himself.'[131] Seeing with the eyes of Christ, Hume gave to priests a precious gift, namely, his time, crucial for any bishop as he states: 'I think one of the most important properties a bishop must have is time. The trouble with most of us is that we have not got time. We have no time to think, to pray, nor have we any time for other people. So we lack that essential commodity which I believe the priests want to find in us which is time, time just to be available.'[132]

There are a number of other occasions both close to home and far away that demonstrate Hume's pastoral gift of *seeing* with the eyes of Christ. Here are a few examples:

On his visits to St Joseph's Hospice in London, Hume said, 'I am nearly always moved by the eyes of those who suffer. So often, despite the pain, the eyes of the sick and dying can convey a remarkable inner peace. It is as if the storm disturbs only the surface of the lake while in the depths there is a stillness and a certain calm. It may indeed be a hard won tranquillity.'[133]

At a Jewish Passover meal, Hume met a woman who had spent some years in a concentration camp. He described his experience: 'But there was one person among those forty who moved me deeply and that was an immensely dignified woman in whose face you could see the marks of suffering.'[134] He related in another publication, 'She was remarkable in her looks, in the strength of her face, and the serenity of her expression.'[135] Honouring the woman's dignity, Hume said, 'My respect for her was enormous as I saw her dignity, and I thought to myself what liberation and freedom have meant to her; not only the liberation she experienced coming out of the concentration camp at the end of the war but when she was joined again to those she loved and who loved her.'[136]

One event that had a profound effect on Hume was a 1984 visit to Ethiopia when a severe famine ravaged the country. Hume recalled encounters whereby both sight and touch led him to contemplate Christ:

> I remember passing an old man lying on the side of the road with many others. Next to him was his wife, and they were both dying. I looked—and this was a moment I shall never forget—into the old man's eyes. We had no language to communicate but I think he guessed in some way that I was a priest and he took my hand and kissed it. I felt very, very small, because in his eyes there was a serenity, peace and human dignity which was very remarkable ... I saw the figure of Christ in him.[137]

Another meeting in Ethiopia when Hume met a small boy bears quoting at length:

> This small boy came up to me and gripped my hand. With his other hand he pointed to his mouth. That was his way of telling me he was very hungry. I said to the interpreter: 'Tell the little boy that I've come here to go home and make certain that food is sent to him.' He went on doing this, but he also got hold of my hand and rubbed it against his cheek. I couldn't understand that, but for the whole hour I was in that camp that little boy wouldn't let go of my hand, and from time to time rubbed it on his cheek. He was very, very hungry ... I remember speaking with that boy and asking him through the interpreter: 'Why are you looking so sad?' and he answered very simply in his own language: 'I am hungry.' I could see in that face the suffering Christ, and I realized just what a terrible scourge

> physical hunger is … Then, when the visit was ended and
> I had to go elsewhere, the little boy stood—I can see him
> now—feet astride, his hands on his waist, and looked at me
> almost with reproach. I could see in his face, 'Why are you
> leaving me behind?' I felt awful because there was no way I
> could take that little boy and bring him back to England.[138]

Hume's experience with the boy led him to contemplate the
Eucharist:

> I realized that when you're lost and are very hungry, and
> you are abandoned, you have a craving for two things:
> for food and for drink and for love … It was the next day
> when I was celebrating Mass that I understood as I've never
> understood before, the secret of Holy Communion. Our
> Lord, realizing how much we need love, how much we
> need to be fed by Him, had this marvellous way of doing
> it: by giving Himself to us.[139]

Hume too gave himself to others, validating their suffering and
their dignity by encountering Christ in their eyes, face, touch,
and presence. By acknowledging each person as made in the
image and likeness of God, Hume raised their suffering, peace,
and even reproach to a supernatural level, the level of meeting
Christ in the Eucharist, as expressed when he summarized his
visit to Ethiopia and the lessons he learned:

> When I visited Ethiopia … I saw clearly how when people
> are abandoned and dying of hunger they crave for love and
> life … I have never forgotten that incident and to this day
> wonder whether that child is still alive. I remember when I
> boarded the helicopter he stood and looked reproachfully.
> An abandoned starving ten year old child … A little
> boy who taught me in a wonderful way something very
> important about going to Holy Communion. I have often
> wondered since what happened to him.[140]

Hume's gift of seeing with the eyes of Christ also helped him
to see the truth in people and events. One significant event was

Hume's involvement in the cases of the Guildford Four and Maguire Seven where he was instrumental in securing the release of wrongly sentenced prisoners. The cases revolved around a series of bombings in English pubs in 1974 that resulted not only in the killing and wounding of innocent people, but also in 'the failure of the British criminal justice system. That failure resulted in the miscarriage of justice for eleven people—the Guildford Four and Maguire Seven. They were all arrested, charged and convicted of being responsible for the bombings, or possessing explosives, and had to remain in prison for many years before their convictions were finally quashed.'[141]

Hume became involved in the cases in 1978 after receiving a letter from one of the accused, Patrick Joseph 'Giuseppe' Conlon, who wrote to Hume from the London prison, Wormwood Scrubs. Conlon was not well, 'suffering from pulmonary tuberculosis and a crippling form of emphysema.'[142] In the letter Conlon pleaded his innocence. It was during a visit to an ailing Conlon in December 1978 that Hume was convinced of his innocence. At the time of Hume's visit, Gerard 'Gerry' Conlon (Giuseppe's son, also accused of the bombings and incarcerated at Wormwood Scrubs) was called from a prison football match to the prison 'movement control'[143] for reasons unknown to him. Gerry Conlon's account reveals the human dimension of his first encounter with Cardinal Hume and Hume seeing with the eyes of Christ through the sense of touch. Gerry Conlon relates, not without a sense of humour, 'So I trundled over to movement control in my football gear, pouring sweat, and all of a sudden I saw this tall thin grey-haired figure waiting for me, wearing a black cape and a red skull-cap, and my first impression was, here was Batman come to see me. Then I heard this screw saying to him, "Your Eminence, this is Conlon."'[144] He continues, 'And the caped figure came up to me and just put his arms around me and said, "I'm Cardinal Hume. Will you take me to see your father?"'[145] After taking Hume to see his father, the younger Conlon expressed his own feelings, his respect for his father, and revealed Hume's gift of seeing with the eyes of Christ:

> Then I felt better, because I knew my father's quality. I knew there was no way Cardinal Hume would not go away convinced that innocent people were in prison … when Cardinal Hume left he said to the screws, 'Make sure you treat these men well, because there may have been a miscarriage of justice.'
>
> And he has continued to say ever since that this meeting was enough to convince him we were innocent, even before he'd seen the evidence.[146]

Regarding Hume's visit to Wormwood Scrubs and Hume's ability to see the truth, Anthony Howard notes, 'one of Basil's small vanities was the pride he took in his intuitive judgment of people. He always made up his mind for himself, and it was when he sat listening to the 54-year-old Giuseppe's story that he first became convinced not only of the truth of what he was being told, but also of the innate honesty of the already seriously ill man who was telling it to him.'[147] Vanity or not, on a spiritual level, the contemplative Hume *looked* for God in events and people. Seeing with the eyes of Christ he gained insight into the truth, especially important in matters of justice, here the imprisonment of innocent people. Patrick Victory also commented on Hume's visit to Conlon:

> This long meeting with Giuseppe Conlon had a profound effect on Cardinal Hume. He was very concerned about the state of the man's health, but also he became deeply aware of the strong likelihood that this man was innocent and there could well have been a miscarriage of justice. As regards the safety of the conviction, the Cardinal knew that he was unable at that time to produce any evidence other than his own judgement.[148]

As a result of Hume's visit with Conlon, Hume wrote a letter to Home Secretary, Merlyn Rees, in March 1979:

My anxiety arises from the fact that there are strong
indications that this man is not guilty of the crime for
which he was convicted …

I have met Mr Conlon myself and would have little
doubt in my own mind that he is innocent …

He is a very sick man and I am very gravely concerned
about the state of his health. This anxiety is shared by
many other persons who are concerned with his case.
He will certainly not live long enough to complete his
sentence. So I am asking you quite frankly for an act of
clemency towards him and that he should be released on
compassionate grounds.[149]

Hume's participation in the case is well expressed by Anne Maguire who was arrested 3 December 1974, and released 22 February 1985, becoming 'the last of the Maguire Seven to be set free,
released from prison'.[150] Maguire relates, 'I believe a turning point
came in the perception of both the public and officialdom when,
above all others, Cardinal Basil Hume, the Archbishop of Westminster, decided to speak out. People, from the highest ranks of
government to the man in the street, knew that he did not lightly
pronounce on matters such as this'.[151] On Hume's visit to Wormwood Scrubs and her high regard for Hume, Maguire comments,

The Cardinal had visited Giuseppe Conlon in prison and
obviously saw that as well as being a sick man, Giuseppe
was a gentle person who wouldn't hurt a fly. When
Giuseppe died still protesting his and our innocence, it
left an impression on the Cardinal. In fact, I cannot speak
highly enough of him. He has done so much to help and
encourage me and all my family that we hold him not only
in great respect but also in love and affection.[152]

In 1989 'the verdicts on the Guildford Four [Patrick Armstrong,
Gerard Conlon, Paul Hill, Carole Richardson] were quashed
and they were released'.[153] A few weeks later Cardinal Hume
paid a pastoral visit to Anne Maguire at her home, where Carol
Richardson and a friend were also visiting. During the course of

the visit, Hume, extending pastoral graciousness, invited them to participate in the Lourdes pilgrimage from Westminster Diocese so that he could show Richardson 'the exact spot where he heard that she had been freed'.[154]

Another recognition of Hume's ability to see the truth appeared in an article in *The Tablet*. The writer quoted Alastair Logan, 'one of the lawyers who fought for the convictions to be overturned'.[155] As related in the article, Logan commented on both Hume and journalist Robert Kee, the author of *Trial and Error*.[156] Logan noted the significance of Kee and Hume being 'convinced of the innocence of the people they had met and talked to'.[157] Logan claimed, 'They could see the truth in other people. The truth was there to be seen and appreciated'.[158]

Hume himself commented on being convinced of Maguire's innocence. As related in the foreword to Maguire's book, *Miscarriage of Justice*, Hume recalls listening to Maguire speak to a group of young people about her story while affirming her dignity and innocence:

> As she told her story they listened to her quite spellbound. It was not so much her story, immensely disquieting as this is, but the quality of the lady who was speaking which impressed them. It was her dignity, her evident goodness and the total lack of bitterness which spoke more eloquently than her words ...
>
> Anne Maguire was caught up in a terrible situation not of her making, accused unjustly of a crime which she never committed. To have met her and to have sat with her in conversation adds to the total improbability of her or any of her family being involved in the terrible crimes of which she was accused.
>
> Anne Maguire never lost her faith in God and in humanity. Perhaps it took this ordeal to bring the best out of her, and she is, as far as I am concerned, a very exceptional woman whom it has been a privilege to get to know.[159]

Reflection

Because Hume was a man dedicated to prayer, he became a great teacher of prayer. A *contemplative* apostle, he found inspiration not only in the Gospel, but also in the saints, and in particular the Northern Saints of England:

> What I admire so much in a person like Saint Aidan—as well as Saint Cuthbert and, indeed, Saint Wilfrid and Saint Hilda, the great abbess—is that these early English saints believed that Jesus revealed God to us, and also revealed the possibility of a relationship with God. They believed it with total conviction. Because they were people who made prayer the essential feature of their lives, it is clear, from studying their lives, that they had been touched by God in some way. There is no doubt in my mind that this combination of faith in the gospel and prayer in their lives transformed them, and led them to become such wonderful instruments of God's love.[160]

Hume, pastor of prayer and pastor at prayer saw the love of God in others and gave love to those he led and taught. Seeing with the eyes of Christ, Hume saw goodness, truth, and beauty in the other. He was the kind of pastor and teacher about whom St Joseph of Calasanza (1557–1648) speaks: 'All who undertake to teach must be endowed with deep love, the greatest patience, and, most of all, profound humility. They must perform their work with earnest zeal. Then through their humble prayers, the Lord will find them worthy to become fellow workers with Him in the cause of truth.'[161] For Hume the quest for truth was absolutely fundamental. He wrote:

> Religion is about truth, truth about God, truth about ourselves. It is truth that makes us free. Saint Bede was a servant of truth. He dedicated his whole life to it. The saints about whom we have been thinking—Paulinus, Aidan, Hilda, Theodore of Tarsus, Benedict Biscop, Wilfrid,

Cuthbert—were all apostles of truth, bringing knowledge of God to the people of their day. In so doing, they were building a society deeply influenced by Christian values.[162]

In our own day, Hume saw society in general and the continent of Europe in particular on a 'spiritual quest',[163] trying to fill 'a void which only the love of God can fill'.[164] He added: Europe 'is in search of its soul, and that soul will only be found when the void is filled by the Gospel in all its simplicity and purity'.[165]

What did Hume himself find after all his searching? Answering this question once in an interview in 1984, he replied: 'I suppose a simpler faith. Deeper. Of course, it isn't all a cloud of unknowing. God has revealed Himself by becoming man.'[166] All of his life Hume challenged himself to grow in spiritual maturity and to deepen his faith through a life of prayer while challenging the faithful to do the same. First, seeking God, and then, by the grace of prayer, learning to become a wonderful communicator and a superb pastor of souls, Hume was a man, a bishop, able to speak of the God whom he knew as a friend with such simplicity and eloquence it was almost as if, like the first visionary teachers of the Gospel, he could 'see the invisible',[167] and announce the Good News with at least something of the grace and authority possessed by those first wise and humble pastors of the Church.

NOTES

[1]   B. Hume, *To Be a Pilgrim: A Spiritual Notebook* (repr. London: SPCK Classics, 2009), p. 49.

[2]   *Ibid.*, p. 25.

[3]   B. Hume, *The Mystery of the Cross*, 2nd ed. (Brewster, MA: Paraclete Press, 2000), p. 4.

[4]   Hume, *To Be a Pilgrim*, p. 38.

[5]   B. Hume, *Footprints of the Northern Saints* (London: Darton, Longman and Todd, 1996), p. 29.

[6]   *Ibid.*, p. 75.

[7]   *Ibid.*, p. 82.

[8]   *Ibid.*, p. 82.

9   *Ibid.*, p. 83.

10   *Ibid.*, p. 91.

11   *Ibid.*

12   Hume, *To Be a Pilgrim*, p. 12.

13   B. Hume, *Cardinal Basil Hume: In My Own Words*, ed. T. de Bertodano (London: Hodder & Stoughton, 1999) p. 83.

14   Hume, *Footprints of the Northern Saints*, p. 82.

15   *Ibid.*

16   B. Hume, *Light in the Lord: Reflections on the Priesthood* (repr. Collegeville: Liturgical Press, 1993), p. 9.

17   *Ibid.*, p. 71.

18   Hume in J. Mortimer, *In Character: Interviews with Some of the Most Influential and Remarkable Men and Women of Our Time* (New York: Penguin Books, 1984), p. 92.

19   A. Convery, interview by author, Ampleforth Abbey, York, 17 September 2013.

20   F. Shand-Kydd, 'A Luminous Simplicity of Expression', in C. Butler, ed., *Basil Hume: By His Friends* (London: Fount, 1999), p. 90.

21   *Ibid.*

22   Hume, *Light in the Lord*, p. 17.

23   *Ibid.*, p. 118.

24   *Ibid.*

25   *Ibid.*, p. 126.

26   Hume, *To Be a Pilgrim*, p. 133.

27   *Ibid.*, p. 218.

28   *Ibid.*

29   Hume, *Light in the Lord*, p. 17.

30   Hume, *To Be a Pilgrim*, p. 133.

31   Mortimer, *In Character*, p. 91.

32   Hume in Mortimer, *In Character*, p. 91.

33   B. Hume, *Basil in Blunderland* (Brewster, MA: Paraclete Press, 1999), p. 9.

34   *Ibid.*

35   *Ibid.*

36   *Ibid.*

37   *Ibid.*

38   C. B. Daly, 'Salute to Cardinal Hume', in Butler, ed. *Basil Hume: By His Friends*, p. 131.

39   A. Roche, 'Foreword', in B. Hume, *A Turning to God*, ed. P. Hardcastle Kelly (Collegeville: Liturgical Press, 2007), p. vii.

40   *Ibid.*

41   *Ibid.*

42   Hume, *Basil in Blunderland*, p. xii.

43   *Ibid.*, p. xi.

44   B. Hume, *The Mystery of Love* (Brewster, MA: Paraclete Press, 2001), p. 43.

45   *Catechism of the Catholic Church* (Libreria Editrice Vaticana: United States Catholic Conference, Inc., 1994), 2559.

46   Hume, *The Mystery of Love*, p. 43.

47   *Ibid.*

48   *Ibid.*, pp. 43–4.

49   Hume, *A Turning to God*, p. 66.

50   Hume, *The Mystery of Love*, p. 22.

51   Hume, *To Be a Pilgrim*, p. 139.

52   B. Hume, *Cardinal Hume: A Spiritual Companion*, 2nd ed. (Brewster, MA: Paraclete Press, 2001), p. 74.

53   Hume, *To Be a Pilgrim*, p. 137.

54   Hume, *Basil in Blunderland*, p. xii.

55   *Ibid.*, p. viii.

56   *Ibid.*, p. xii.

57   *Ibid.*

58   *Ibid.*

59   *Ibid.*, p. xiii.

60   *Ibid.*

61   Hume, *Light in the Lord*, p. 84.

62   B. Hume, unpublished conference, 23 October 1973, used with permission of the Ampleforth Abbey Trust, York.

63   *Ibid.*

64   *Ibid.*

65   *Ibid.*

66   Hume, *Basil in Blunderland*, p. xiii.

67   *Ibid.*

68   *Ibid.*

69   *Ibid.*

70   B. Hume, *The Mystery of the Cross* (Brewster, MA: Paraclete Press, 2000), p. 47.

71   Hume, *Basil in Blunderland*, p. 59.

72   *Ibid.*, p. xiv.

73   *Ibid.*

74   *Ibid.*

75 *Ibid.*

76 *Ibid.*

77 *Ibid.*

78 *Ibid.*

79 *Ibid.*

80 *Ibid.*

81 *Ibid.*

82 *Ibid.*

83 Hume, *To Be a Pilgrim*, pp. 69–70.

84 Hume, *Basil in Blunderland*, pp. xiv-xv.

85 *Ibid.*, p. xv.

86 *Ibid.*

87 *Ibid.*

88 Hume, *The Mystery of Love*, p. 19.

89 *Ibid.*

90 *Ibid.*

91 *Ibid.*

92 Hume, *Basil in Blunderland*, p. 30.

93 *Ibid.*, p. 32.

94 *Ibid.*

95 *Ibid.*, p. xv.

96 *Ibid.*

97 *Ibid.*

98 *Ibid.*

99 *Ibid.*

100 *Ibid.*

101 *Ibid.*, pp. xv-xvi.

102 *Ibid.*, p. xvi.

103 *Ibid.*

104 *Ibid.*

105 Hume, *To Be a Pilgrim*, p. 129.

106 *Ibid.*

107 Hume, *Basil in Blunderland*, p. xvi.

108 *Ibid.*

109 *Ibid.*

110 Hume, *The Mystery of the Cross*, pp. 49–50.

111 Hume, *Basil in Blunderland*, p. xvii.

112 *Ibid.*, p. 6.

[113] *Ibid.*, pp. 6–7.

[114] *Ibid.*, p. 6.

[115] *Ibid.*, p. 7.

[116] *Ibid.*

[117] B. Hume, *Searching for God* (New York: Paulist Press, 1978), p. 100.

[118] Hume, *Basil in Blunderland*, p. xiii.

[119] Hume, *To Be a Pilgrim*, p. 112.

[120] *Ibid.*

[121] Hume, *Cardinal Basil Hume: In My Own Words*, p. 106.

[122] F. Lawrence and Children, 'An Indefinable Quietude', in Butler, ed., *Basil Hume: By His Friends*, p. 128.

[123] Pope Benedict XVI, Encyclical *Deus Caritas Est*, 18.

[124] Hume, *Light in the Lord*, p. 142.

[125] V. Guazzelli, 'Archbishop and Pastoral Leader', in T. Castle, ed., *Basil Hume: A Portrait* (London: Fount, 1987), p. 90.

[126] *Ibid.*, pp. 90–1.

[127] W. Charles, ed. *Basil Hume: Ten Years On* (London: Burns & Oates, 2009), p. 89.

[128] Guazzelli, 'Archbishop and Pastoral Leader', in Castle, ed., *Basil Hume: A Portrait*, p. 91.

[129] *Ibid.*

[130] *Ibid.*

[131] *Ibid.*

[132] Hume, *Light in the Lord*, p. 143.

[133] Hume, *The Mystery of the Cross*, p. 51.

[134] Hume, *Light in the Lord*, pp. 108–109.

[135] B. Hume, *The Mystery of the Incarnation* (Brewster, MA: Paraclete Press, 2000), p. 114.

[136] Hume, *Light in the Lord*, p. 109.

[137] Hume in Charles, ed., *Basil Hume: Ten Years On*, p. 176.

[138] *Ibid.*, pp. 177–178.

[139] *Ibid.*, p. 178.

[140] *Ibid.*

[141] P. Victory, *Justice and Truth: The Guildford Four and Maguire Seven* (London: Sinclair-Stevenson, 2002), p. 1.

[142] Victory, *Justice and Truth*, p. 14.

[143] G. Conlon, *In the Name of the Father* (London: Plume, 1993), p. 185.

[144] *Ibid.*, pp. 185–6.

[145] *Ibid.*, p. 186.

[146] *Ibid.*

[147] A. Howard, *Basil Hume: The Monk Cardinal* (London: Headline Book Publishing, 2006), p. 170.

[148] Victory, *Justice and Truth*, pp. 14–15.

[149] Hume in Victory, *Justice and Truth*, pp. 15–16.

[150] Victory, *Justice and Truth*, pp. xii, xv.

[151] A. Maguire with J. Gallagher, *Miscarriage of Justice: An Irish Family's Story of Wrongful Conviction as IRA Terrorists* (Niwot, CO: Roberts Rinehart Publishers, 1994), pp. 145–6.

[152] *Ibid.*, 146.

[153] *Ibid.*

[154] *Ibid.*, p. 147.

[155] 'Cardinal Hume's Fight for Justice', *The Tablet* (22 June 2002), p. 31.

[156] See R. Kee, *Trial and Error: The Maguires, the Guildford Pub Bombers and British Justice* (London: Penguin Books, 1989).

[157] A. Logan in 'Cardinal Hume's Fight for Justice', p. 31.

[158] *Ibid.*

[159] Hume, 'Foreword', in Maguire, *Miscarriage of Justice*, p. vi.

[160] Hume, *Footprints of the Northern Saints*, pp. 81–2.

[161] St Joseph of Calasanza in R. De Sola Chervin, compiler, *Quotable Saints* (Ann Arbor, MI: Servant Publications, 1992), p. 57.

[162] Hume, *Footprints of the Northern Saints*, p. 92.

[163] B. Hume, *Remaking Europe: The Gospel in a Divided Continent* (London: Society for Christian Knowledge, 1994), p. x.

[164] *Ibid.*, p. xi.

[165] *Ibid.*

[166] Hume in Mortimer, *In Character*, p. 91.

[167] Pope Paul VI, Apostolic Exhortation *Evangelii Nuntiandi*, 76.

Chapter 4

Hume the Preacher

Suffering, the Cross, Death, Resurrection

THE THEME OF THE CROSS appears regularly throughout the preaching and teaching of Basil Hume. Early in
his years as abbot, Hume, almost astoundingly, told the
Community at Ampleforth, 'It is remarkable that in the Gospel,
as far as I remember, Our Lord does not talk about following
Him or being His disciples without a reference to the Cross or
to the chalice, the symbol of suffering.'[1] One can infer from such
a declaration that discipleship does not come without suffering
and the Cross, a truth Jesus pronounced: 'Whoever wishes to
come after me must deny himself, take up his cross, and follow
me' (Mt 16:24). For anyone interested in deepening their spiritual
life, the Cross cannot be avoided, made clear by Hume: 'There
is no spiritual maturity without the Cross. If you don't meet the
Cross some time in your life you can never be spiritually mature:
you remain spiritually a child.'[2]

Accepting the Cross as part and parcel of the spiritual journey,
the pilgrim searching for God remembers that he or she does not
choose which cross will be carried. Hume told the Community,
'we never tailor our own crosses: we don't carve our own crosses
to fit our own shoulders: it's always the one that rubs just where
it hurts; it's never the cross of my choosing.'[3] Be that as it may in
whatever form the Cross may take, the form of 'misunderstandings, an unearned rebuke, gnawing anxiety, ill-health, fatigue',[4]
each person makes a choice, 'decide[s] whether these are obsta-

cles to happiness or a path leading to it.'[5] Looking to Christ in
the Garden of Gethsemane, who 'recoiled from the Passion, but
accepted it willingly—more than that, lovingly',[6] we are called
to accept our crosses. They lead to happiness—they are means
whereby one shares in the risen life of Christ, for 'The Cross
on its own does not make sense. The Cross together with the
Resurrection does.'[7]

As abbot, Hume prepared the monastic community for the
Lenten season by elaborating on chapter 49 of the Rule of St
Benedict, 'The Observance of Lent'. Hume unpacked what he
called the 'ascetical'[8] aspect of Lent, that is, 'we urge the entire
community during these days of Lent to keep its manner of life
most pure and to wash away in this holy season the negligences
of other times.'[9]

Developing the ascetical, the aspect of Lent most clearly
associated with the Passion of Our Lord, Hume speaks of the
value and purpose of suffering on three levels: ascetical, mystical, and participatory. At the same time Hume keeps in mind St
Benedict's other 'directive for the observance of Lent—to look
forward to the coming of Easter'.[10] Hume suggested that minds
should dwell on the holy feast of Easter, 'the central act of the
redemptive work of our blessed Lord.'[11] Easter, that is, Resurrection, provides the context in which one looks at the ascetical
aspect of Lent. Suffering by means of ascetical practices, 'The
Christian has to be constantly making a personal response to the
mystery of Christ. He has constantly to take steps to die to this
world, in order to live more effectively the life of the risen Christ,
a life hidden in Christ with God.'[12] While reminding one of his
or her frailty, these ascetical practices are essential for anyone
desiring to share in the Resurrection, as Hume said, 'the sharing
of the risen life of Christ has to be worked out within the context
of the Passion.'[13]

The Purpose and Value of Suffering

Many carry crosses and share in the Passion of Christ in, as Hume said, 'very small ways, each day; the various difficulties, contradictions, misunderstandings, and so forth, and at times there can be long periods of stress and strain—periods of sadness and sorrow, in which we are truly living the Passion of Christ in our lives'.[14] Whether in small doses or large, sharing in the Passion can lead to darkness and depression. It is only through the eyes of faith that anyone can seek to understand that suffering has purpose and value. Hume reveals the purpose and value of suffering: 'it has a value precisely because Christ has risen from the dead, precisely because He has overcome all that is negative in suffering, and given it particular value, since each sharing in the Passion of Christ leads to greater sharing in the life of His Resurrection.'[15] In other words, while recognizing the need for grace, 'suffering experienced leads, when accepted and borne in a true Christian spirit, to an increase in grace'.[16]

Suffering at the Ascetical Level

Suffering is ascetical: 'At the ascetical level: suffering detaches us from living only for this world, it saves us from deceiving ourselves into thinking that achievement in this world is the thing that really matters, and reminds us that our treasure is in heaven.'[17] Achieving great things in earthly life, seemingly on our efforts alone, does not lead to fulfilment and peace, as the author of the Book of Ecclesiastes makes clear: 'All things are vanity!' (Qo 1:2). Better is to suffer through failures and mistakes and make space for grace. Open to the gift of grace, one is enabled to grow in spiritual maturity and continue the pilgrim journey to God. Hume commented on the honour of encountering such a person who has grown through mistakes: 'When you meet a person who has made a mistake in life, or people who have made lots of mistakes, and this has made them truly humble, then you can see the grace of God beginning to work, and it is a great privilege to have encountered that.'[18] The voice of God speaks through all crosses—difficulties, failures, mistakes—through all that one suffers and endures. Suffering by carrying one's cross puts one in touch with reality, helps the pilgrim to focus on the search for God instead of earthly achievement, clearly stated by Hume: 'Every difficulty in life is a call from God to turn one's attention to Him, and to find in Him the ultimate meaning of our lives.'[19]

Suffering at the Mystical Level

Suffering 'is purposeful at a mystical level: by meditating on the Passion of Christ we grow in sympathy for, and understanding of what He did for us.'[20] In prayerful meditation, we probe the *mystery* of the Passion. Hume defined *mystery* as 'a truth that lies beyond our understanding.'[21] Furthermore, a mystery 'lies beyond us; it is too rich for our understanding. It can be entered into, explored, even inhabited; but it can never be exhausted or fathomed.'[22] We will never fully understand what Christ experienced but that should not stop us from striving for growth, both in sympathy and understanding.

The same is true for those sharing the sufferings of another. One will never fully understand the experience of the other, but walking with the other 'draws one even more closely to that person',[23] vital in all pastoral situations. As Hume stated, 'Hearing or listening to someone telling us about an experience which we have not shared makes us respond with sympathy, we grow in understanding of that person.'[24] Moreover, 'one grows closer to people when there is sharing in suffering, when there is sharing in the same experience.'[25] Practically speaking, another way for those involved in pastoral care to grow closer to the Lord and to the other, is to 'look at the Cross and see in that figure one's own relations, friends, and pastoral concerns.'[26] Hume suggests starting 'with one's own family; go through the different members of it, and practically in every case you can find some aspect, or some problem in their lives which, if I can use these terms, qualifies them to be where Our Lord is as we look at the Cross.'[27] Taking one's own problems and the problems of others to the Lord on the Cross in contemplative prayer leads to peace, not frustration, for Christ crucified is the power of God and the wisdom of God (see 1 Co 1:24). Relying on the wisdom and power of God helps to make sense of suffering while opening one to the gift of grace. In the midst of suffering, the Holy Spirit is active, for 'the experience of human emptiness and human limitation at a spiritual level is a void which can only be filled by the Holy Spirit.'[28]

Suffering at the Participatory Level

At this level, Hume recalls the much-pondered phrase of St Paul in his letter to the Colossians: 'Now I rejoice in my sufferings for your sake, and in my flesh I am filling up what is lacking in the afflictions of Christ on behalf of His body, which is the Church' (Col 1:24). Hume reflects, the phrase 'does seem to mean at least this much: that Our Lord wants us to be associated in His redemptive act.'[29] Christ, seated at the right hand of the Father, no longer undergoes suffering, or experiences His Passion. The members of Christ's body now have a responsibility to 'prolong His Passion in the world—in order to prolong His redemptive act, because the redeeming act of Christ is not something that just happened in the past, it is a fact now.'[30] On an earlier occasion, Hume noted: 'We become involved in what was in the first instance an historical fact, but now through the Ascension has received its eternal dimension. An event which is ever present. In that event we become involved, first through baptism and then every time that those signs which are the sacraments are done before us or with us.'[31] Hume echoed this teaching in 1975: 'So often we can look at Christ's redemptive work as something which took place at a moment in history, the fruits of which are applied to us and principally through the sacraments. What is applied is new life which should bring joy and enthusiasm to all.'[32]

Hume spoke of another level of participation. Christ's work of redemption 'has to be in some measure an inner experience.'[33] With faith, Christians, together with 'all people of good will in whose hearts grace is secretly at work'[34] *encounter* or 'experience the life of Christ within us, that strange life of the resurrected Christ which is a mixture of a life of the crucified and the life of the risen, the co-existence of suffering and pain with joy and serenity, that complex situation in which we are as redeemed persons, not yet in possession of that complete joy, complete serenity, which will be ours at the beatific vision.'[35] One might say that an alliance with Christ has been forged. In the depths of being, the Body of Christ cooperates with Christ the Head: 'Associated with Him, and in Him,'[36] the Church has a role to play: 'He, the head, risen and ascended is there preparing for us that place in Heaven which is ours, if we respond and associate ourselves with His life, and that includes His Passion.'[37]

At three levels of suffering: ascetical, mystical, and participatory, the 'call to share in the Passion, is loud and compelling.'[38] All are moved to 'a more wholehearted response to the call of God—a more wholehearted response to the command to take up our cross and follow Our Blessed Lord—as a condition for entering into a closer relation with Him',[39] and subsequently a condition for entering into closer relation with others. Hence the purpose of the Cross: 'Everything in the Christian life, and therefore in the monastic life, is ordered to charity, and charity is concerned with loving other people'.[40]

As one *surrenders* mind and heart in faith, the grace of God begins to work. As seen in Church teaching, the living and true God on the Cross, in His suffering and death 'not only set an example for us to follow in His footsteps, but He also opened for us a way in which life and death are sanctified and given fresh significance'.[41] The *encounter* with the Passion and Resurrection

of Christ associates us with His redemptive act, 'the work of salvation He has wrought on your behalf and mine',[42] whereby we
are enabled to carry on His work of redemption, drawing closer
to the Lord and to others in suffering. All is gift, all is privilege
as 'effectiveness in our work will depend on being filled with the
Spirit who gives us the power and the wisdom of God which
comes from a daily effort in union with Christ Our Lord',[43] the
encounter of love meeting love.

The Last Words of Jesus

Seven times He spoke
Seven words of love
And all three hours His silence cried
For mercy on the souls of men
Jesus, our Lord, is crucified.

Frederick William Faber,
'O Come and Mourn with Me Awhile'

These words from Faber's hymn are a fitting introduction to Cardinal Hume's meditations on the last words of Jesus. The 'seven words of love' speak of the last words Jesus uttered while hanging on the Cross.

'Father, forgive them, they know not what they do'
   (Lk 23:34).
'Amen, I say to you, today you will be with me in Paradise'
   (Lk 23:43).
'Woman, behold, your son ... Behold, your mother'
   (Jn 19:26–7).
'My God, my God, why have You forsaken me?'
   (Mk 15:34).
'I thirst' (Jn 19:28).
'It is finished' (Jn 19:30).
'Father, into Your hands I commend my spirit' (Lk 23:46).

Basil Hume delivered his first meditations on the last words of Jesus in 1963, just after his fortieth birthday and shortly before he was elected Abbot of Ampleforth. The occasion was a visit by the Edinburgh String Quartet to the Abbey Church, where they performed Franz Joseph Hadyn's *The Seven Last Words of Christ on the Cross*. As related in the *Ampleforth Journal*: 'This work, written in 1785 for the Holy Week Services in Cadiz Cathedral [Spain], was performed in its original form, with a short discourse by a priest after each "word", followed by a short piece of music.'[44]

The priest was Basil Hume. The 1963 meditations reveal Hume's spiritual maturity. He embraced the Cross early in his monastic life and continued to do so through his years as Abbot and Cardinal. In the pages that follow, new meditations are developed through the previously unpublished 1963 meditations and later published works, mainly *Hope from the Cross: Reflections on Jesus' Seven Last Words*. In the Preface of that work, Liam Kelly writes, 'On a number of occasions, Cardinal Hume gave reflections on the Seven Last Words of Christ ... Within them, he once said, there is "a message of hope, an Easter gift which gives meaning to Good Friday's agony." These texts are gathered here to share that message of hope in a new future.'[45] Emphasizing the intensity of Christ's last words, Hume said, 'Each of these "last words" has the power to transform the lives of you and me, for they are the word of God ... Let those words speak to you and I will tell you what they have said to me.'[46]

Father, forgive them for they know not what they do

> He forgave because he loved
> Love is the whole explanation
> of all he did.
> Love it was that made him live
> like us
> And experience
> Suffering and death
> All things human
> have different meaning now
> Suffering—to purify
> Death the gateway to life.
> Because thou Lord didst suffer
> and die
> For us.
> How little we understand,
> How insensitive
> ungrateful
> Forgive us, we know not what we do[47]

Father, forgive them for they know not what they do. Reflecting on these words, one may ask: How often am I blind, oblivious, or numb to the wounds I inflict on God, myself, and others through neglect, ignorance, self-centredness, abuse of power, or ambition? Like the Roman soldiers who 'were degrading themselves more than him',[48] we too exhibit 'man's inhumanity to man.'[49] Personalizing Christ's *word*, Hume commented, '"We do not know what we do"—that word is profound.'[50] 'How little we understand, how insensitive ungrateful'[51] we are.

On this word Hume reflected, 'The human voice of the Lord in His agony shows ... a divine generosity that is surprising, and so very consoling.'[52] Sadly, one often becomes overburdened with guilt, fixating on sin and wrong-doing while forgetting the words of the psalmist: 'Merciful and gracious is the Lord, slow to anger, abounding in kindness' (Ps 103:8). Hume commented on the pleasing taste of this word: '"Father, forgive them ..." Were there ever words so sweet to the ears of those burdened and weighed down by wrongdoing and sin?'[53] Hume reminds us, 'There is a deeper truth for us to learn. It is that God always seeks to forgive; He will look for every reason to forgive, to make excuses for us, to understand.'[54]

A second aspect of Our Lord's divine generosity is 'God's forgiveness ... the faithful companion of sorrow.'[55] By acknowledging wrong-doing, expressing sorrow, and humbly asking for forgiveness, one assumes responsibility for one's thoughts, words, and actions. We seek healing in Christ's words: *Forgive them for they know not what they do.* The offended continues to seek healing. The offender accepts the Lord's forgiveness. Our Lord on the Cross provides healing. 'Nonetheless', Hume stated, God 'looks into our hearts to find "sorrow" or at least the beginnings of it. He expects us to be sorry, and to say so, to recognize the wrong we have done',[56] however painful it may be to utter the words.

Like the forgiveness of Christ, forgiveness should be all-encompassing, clearly articulated by Hume: 'do not ever withhold your smile of forgiveness, even when they do not know what they do.'[57] If 'love is the whole explanation of all [Jesus] did',[58] for 'He forgave because He loved',[59] then love should become the whole explanation of all we do. 'To forgive is a lovely quality in God. It is equally lovely among ourselves.'[60] With Jesus' words of forgiveness, we are set free to forgive, ask for forgiveness, and be forgiven, even when the wounds and hurts run deep, scarring our hearts. Therefore, we face our true selves and pray with Cardinal Hume: 'Father, forgive me; I do not know what I do. I do not know what I have done. But, Lord, is that entirely so? Is there not within me that uneasy feeling in which a voice speaks, a voice difficult to hear now because so often unheeded, a voice that speaks of reproach?'[61] Humbly and making no excuses we heed the voice that 'calls for a response by me; not a protest, not a curse, not a cry, but a prayer, one that pierces His heart so that love may flow from it—just one word: *Sorry.*'[62] Yes, 'There is comfort in remembering that a humble and contrite heart he will not spurn.'[63] *Father, forgive them for they know not what they do.*

Amen I say to you,
This day you will be with me in paradise

> For the thief,
> So much suffering,
> brutal punishment,
> The gnawing anxiety of a mis-spent life;
> nothing now but darkness and death;
> Then the simple reassuring words.
> Bewildered first
> Unbelieving
> He slowly finds light and life;
> No terror now in pain,
> his heart is at peace,
> his mind at rest
> and his dying lips
> bless his new-found Master
> The author of life.[64]

Amen I say to you, this day you will be with me in paradise. The entry-way to this last word of Jesus is the request of the criminal who said, 'Jesus, remember me when You come into Your Kingdom' (Lk 23:42). Acknowledging his wrong-doing, expressing sorrow, and seeking forgiveness, the good thief pleads with the Lord: Do not forget me! He took a risk, anxious about how Christ might respond to his request. Still, he 'dared to believe'[65] in the 'love of God'[66] and His 'goodness'.[67] 'Sad, sorry, repentant, broken almost,'[68] with 'gnawing anxiety of a mis-spent life; nothing now but darkness and death',[69] the thief 'sought to make amends.'[70] Remember me, Lord.

The thief was 'abandoned with no family to comfort nor friends to help'.[71] Perhaps he did turn to others for help, but 'Who remembers a common thief, dying on a cross for the wrong he has done? Who will stand by him, claim his friendship?'[72] In their fickleness, his family and friends turned away, an echo of Jesus' relatives who declared, 'He is out of His mind' (Mk 3:21). The thief turned to 'his new-found Master the author of life',[73] the One also deserted, the One 'spurned and avoided by others' (Is 53:3). 'Then the simple reassuring words',[74] *today you will be with me in paradise*. 'This day—could he have expected that?'[75] 'Bewildered first unbelieving he slowly finds light and life'.[76] 'This day—when his final agony came, he was at peace. Death came, not a foe, but a gentle friend.'[77] So *apropos* is the wisdom of St Benedict: never 'turn away when someone needs your love';[78] 'Go to help the troubled and console the sorrowing.'[79] Here is another example of God's divine generosity: 'Others may ignore, forget, lose interest. He never does.'[80] God's mercy and forgiveness know no bounds, better expressed by Hume, '[God] wants us, wants us more than we have ever wanted Him, or ever could.'[81]

With the soothing and comforting words of the Lord, the thief, 'his heart ... at peace, his mind at rest',[82] would share Christ's joy completely (see Jn 17:13). Each time we receive the Eucharist with the words: 'Lord, I am not worthy that You should enter under my roof, but only say the word and my soul shall be healed',[83] remember Hume's words of comfort, 'Yesterday's thief can be tomorrow's saint.'[84] Renewed in hope, we turn to Him, for 'indeed the Lord assures us in His love: I do not wish the death of the sinner, but that he turn back to me and live.'[85] 'Do not despair nor give up hope; however far you may have wandered, whatever wrong you may have done, despair must never be a word for you.'[86] '"This day you will be with me in paradise," it will be said to you when you have prayed, "Remember me ..."'[87] 'But remember, too, the words, "Father, forgive them; they do not know what they are doing." They are addressed to us when our hearts are humble and contrite, or at least we want to be so. To know that is to experience, even now, the joy that will be fully ours in paradise.'[88] *Amen I say to you, this day you will be with me in paradise.*

Woman, behold thy son, Thou behold thy mother

> His hour had come
> And hers too;
> She had given him life;
> Now she stands and watches,
> As life slowly and painfully
> leaves him.
> The sight of it
> pierces like a sword
> Her mother's heart.
> This is her hour of agony,
> one with his.
> Her pains
> make her mother again,
> of sinful humans
> born to newness of life
> in the death of her son.[89]

Woman behold thy son, Thou behold thy mother. Mary pondered these words as she pondered the angel Gabriel's greeting: 'Hail, favoured one! The Lord is with you' (Lk 1:28–9). With her response, 'Let it be done to me according to your word' (Lk 1:38), Mary invites us to make her words our own. Mary invites us to share with her in the suffering of her Son. 'His hour had come and hers too.'[90]

In Mary's pain, in our pain, in the pain of the other, realize 'that every pain and each trial is a call from God to each one personally to become holy, to draw closer to Him.'[91] We draw closer to Jesus by standing with His Mother: 'Now she stands and watches, as life slowly and painfully leaves Him,'[92] she 'noble, dignified, courageous, strong. *Stabat Mater*, the mother stood.'[93] 'Mary stood with John, with Mary and Salome, too, a mother mourning her son, suffering, sharing His pain.'[94] 'Her soul pierced by the sword of suffering—as Simeon foretold—as if in labour she was now

mother again, Mother of the Church, Mother of those reborn in
the font of baptism and nourished by His body and blood, the
water and blood that came from the wound in His side.'[95]

To John, the beloved disciple, Jesus commands, 'Behold, your
mother' (Jn 19:27). There is mutual beholding between John
and Mary. John would 'provide for her needs as she would provide for his, a space for her in his home perhaps'.[96] Yet there is a
deeper level to the space that John would provide, 'most surely
a space for her in his heart.'[97] Mary too has space for John in her
heart—she has space in her heart for all 'sinful humans born to
newness of life in the death of her son.'[98] *Woman behold thy son,
Thou behold thy mother.*

My God, My God why hast Thou forsaken me?

> He has been stripped of all,
> but who minds being stripped
> if God be still possessed?
> This is the most frightening moment.
> For he suffers now
> the desolation
> of abandonment,
> the hideous emptiness
> of life without God.
> A great mystery.
> We cannot understand.
> A great consolation, though,
> For those called to share this trial
> in the depths of human sadness
> and great darkness of soul,
> When death is more welcome
> than life,
> Self no longer counts.
> The soul finds God,
> rather
> is found by him—
> and lives[99]

My God, my God why hast Thou forsaken me? 'He has been stripped of all, but who minds being stripped if God is still possessed? This is the most frightening moment. For He suffers now the desolation of abandonment, the hideous emptiness of life without God.'[100] In these words, we probe deeper and deeper the *mystery* of the Passion with Cardinal Hume: 'How He who was God could experience such pain, know such abandonment, such emptiness, we do not know. We can only ponder upon the fact in silent prayer.'[101] It may be that we are called to share in Christ's suffering. 'We may be sick or handicapped; we may realize that we are old and unloved; we may have been deserted or let down; we may be out of work and losing our pride.'[102] 'When in the mind there is only darkness and fear, when there is only emptiness and none to help or console. When life has only death to offer to escape from pain and to be at rest. Then we cry out in anguish to God to come to help, to console.'[103] United with the Lord in a cry to the Father: *My God, my God, why have You forsaken me?* Why so much suffering, why so much pain? 'At times of great distress and confusion, thinking may only add to the pain, and praying will be impossible. Then the only helpful thing, the only possible thing, is to sit or kneel looking at the crucifix, the image of Christ dying on the Cross.'[104]

It is a 'great mystery. We cannot understand. A great consolation, though, for those called to share this trial in the depths of human sadness and great darkness of soul.'[105] We are united in darkness. 'His darkest moment, and ours, is one darkness. Into that darkness comes His light, not ours, but given to us to be our peace.'[106] In darkness, Christ is with us as we search for light and pray, 'Look upon me, answer me, Lord, my God! Give light to my eyes lest I sleep in death' (Ps 13:4). It is a 'gift when all is darkness, emptiness too, is precious in the eyes of a Father who seeks above all our trusting of Him when that trust is hard to give. Give it, and the emptiness is filled, inner wounds healed, and peace achieved.'[107]

In the end, 'We can do no more than just look at the crucifix—but we can do no better, for then it will give up its "secret." It will speak to us—in our misery—of hope and encouragement. There is no tidy, rational explanation for the crushing burden of suffering. We cannot work out easy answers to why it should be.'[108] It is the Cross that will reveal the answer, 'but it has to be a personal discovery. You cannot begin to see pattern and purpose unless you have known the Cross and blindly let Jesus lead you from despair into hope.'[109] *My God, my God why hast Thou forsaken me?* 'It was His prayer as He trod the pilgrim way, through despair and the dark vale of tears and anguish to that hope: God's gift to those who feel forsaken. It is then that they must abandon their hearts to Him when they see no point in so doing.'[110] At last, 'the soul finds God, rather is found by him—and lives'.[111] *My God, my God why hast Thou forsaken me?*

I thirst

He longs for
parched lips to be moistened
his aching thirst to be slaked;
Less a pain that
than the sorrow of love ignored,
Kindness spurned.
He had longed
To give much.
No bitterness
only sadness
loneliness
He has drunk the chalice of sorrow.
They quench now
with vinegar and gall.[112]

I thirst. For Hume, these words were 'of all the last words that He spoke on the Cross the most personal and the most intimate.'[113] Hume re-emphasizes the theme of God's search for us, and ours for God, one that is mutual and intimate. In this word, Christ revealed His initiative of love, a 'divine thirst,'[114] that is, 'God's thirst for you and me.'[115] *I thirst.* 'It is the revelation of God's great love, at once warm and strong, for us and for those of us also who have rejected or despised Him.'[116] It is in these words, Hume said, that we touch 'upon the mystery that is the secret He would wish to share with you and me. He thirsts for us and, perhaps, especially for those who feel the most abandoned. God thirsts for man's love, and that thirst can only be satisfied when we have begun to thirst and hunger for him. He longs for me. He thirsts.'[117]

Thirsting, we sing with the psalmist: 'As the deer longs for streams of water, so my soul thirsts for You, O God. My being thirsts for God, the living God. When can I go and see the face of God?' (Ps 42:2–3). And again, 'O God, You are my God—for You I long! For You my body yearns; for You my soul thirsts,

Like a land parched, lifeless, and without water' (Ps 63:2). Hume responds, 'I long, I yearn, I thirst. Those words belong, surely, to the language of love. To long for the beloved, to yearn, to pine for the beloved—to be thirsty.'[118] This language of love is foreign to many so we ask with Hume, 'Do I truly yearn? Is there pining in my heart for You? Do I thirst?'[119] Now questioning, it is time to listen to the still small voice of the Lord: '*Come closer. Linger in prayer at the foot of the Cross and listen, for I have a word to speak into your ear. This is my word: I thirst.* My tongue is parched—the terrible thirst of a dying man with a longing for a drink that will quench my thirst ... Follow me in your thoughts and prayers; then you, too, will begin to long for me, to yearn, to pine, to thirst.'[120]

Christ was thirsty on two levels. On the physical level 'He was thirsty, His lips dry, His palate parched, He longed to drink',[121] for 'His aching thirst to be slaked'.[122] More painful though was 'the sorrow of love ignored, kindness spurned',[123] this the pain of betrayal. 'He had been betrayed by His friend, by Judas. He had been rejected by His own, those who had supported Him. Judas, oh Judas—betrayal hurts more when the one who betrays has received much from the one he betrays. Betrayal hurts, hurts very much.'[124] Even so the Lord still thirsts for our love, for intimacy with us 'who can so easily betray or at least lose our way by forgetting or ignoring Him who thirsts for you and me.'[125] 'His human heart pined for all of us and still does.'[126] There is one way to quench that thirst, 'A sweet cooling drink—our gift of love—to quench the thirst of Him who first loved us.'[127] For Hume this is 'true love',[128] this 'the meeting of two thirsts—I thirst for you, you thirst for me. Then the stream runs and the land is no longer dry and weary without water, for the streams are running, the ones that flow from heart to heart.'[129] *I thirst.*

It is finished

He has completed the work
given him by the Father;
Soon he will be glorified
with that glory
which was his
before the world began—
The Son of God
True God and True man.
Man's debt to God is paid;
The wrongs wrought by sin
are now put right;
Human nature in him
passes through death to life,
and itself will share
the glory of God—
inherit the Kingdom,
His work is done—
he leaves his followers
to tread like him
the way to Calvary;
Sustained by him
and guided,
each one makes his way to God.[130]

It is finished. '*Consummatum est*—it is achieved, it is completed.'[131] 'Obedient to His Father's will,'[132] 'He has completed the work given Him by the Father; soon He will be glorified with that glory which was His before the world began.'[133] Breathless, Christ struggles physically to exhale, to utter His final words of life, joy, and love. Mysteriously, 'He has hidden in human pain the seed of divine life. Hope is now hidden in human despair, joy concealed in human sadness.'[134] United with Christ and in faith, minds and hearts *surrender* with 'the conviction that there is a reality that is above and beyond our limited human minds, truths that we could not discover ourselves.'[135] Pointing to Christ for understanding and comfort, Hume asks: 'You know suffering? So did He. Have you felt abandoned? And abandoned by God too? So did He. Have you been humiliated, despised, insulted? So was He. You have been misunderstood, vilified? So was He. He, too, walked in the dark, entered the tomb lifeless and defeated, vanquished.'[136] Still 'Death could not win. His body would not be imprisoned.'[137] 'Human nature in him passes through death to life, and itself will share the glory of God.'[138]

In His work of redemption, the Lord took 'our pain and death as well—upon Himself.'[139] 'Man's debt to God is paid; the wrongs wrought by sin are now put right'.[140] 'He has made all things new. It is finished. The work is done.'[141] But humanity's work is not. Humanity has a responsibility to share in and prolong Christ's work of redemption, Christ 'leaves His followers to tread like Him the way to Calvary; sustained by him and guided, each one makes his way to God.'[142] 'There will still be suffering, earthquakes, wars and famine, mental anguish, anxiety, loss of reason, still part of human living, but different now.'[143] All 'hide within themselves a rich reward, a precious treasure—life hidden with Christ in God for the sharers in His Passion.'[144]

We will never fully understand Christ's redemptive work. It is 'Not for me to read the mind of God, nor to pronounce on His ways. Much is hidden, little revealed. And yet, though hard at times to see, love is His reason. This and only this inspires His deeds.'[145] *Consummatum est.* 'The Lord has touched our human experience and leads it now through the darkness to light, from death to life ... to a life of which there is no end and where the desires of humans are finally and completely fulfilled ... a happiness given to those who have sought, only and above all, that His will be done. For such His work is completed and brought to perfection.'[146] *It is finished.*

Father, into thy hands I commend my spirit

The last moment has come
They can hurt him no more
He has passed already
Beyond the pains of this world
Serene
Peaceful
Full of joy
He gives himself
in his last breath
Back to the hands
that first fashioned the earth's dust
into man
They will take him down
and bury him,
But the tomb of death
will not hold captive
the giver of life.
Not for him the return to dust,
but the triumph of
Resurrection.[147]

Into Your hands I commit my spirit. This was Jesus Christ's prayer at the last moment, repeated down the ages by men and women, tortured and killed for their beliefs, the martyrs. That prayer has been said by countless men and women lying sick in the hospital; martyrs, too, in their way: by parents mourning a child; by lovers broken by their parting from each other; by people tortured by anxiety and worry—by men and women of great courage and endless patience, all of them masters of their pain and sorrow because disciples of their suffering Lord.[148]

Father, into Thy hands I commend my spirit. 'The end was near. He was in great distress, overcome by pain, His mind in turmoil. He had no choice but to abandon Himself into the outstretched hands of His heavenly Father.'[149] For Hume, these words are 'the password into His presence, into those hands, safe hands, stretching out to receive His weary soul.'[150] These words are the password for all who suffer abuse, illness, a broken heart, or emotional distress. The call is clear to all who suffer with the Lord: reach out and take firm hold of those hands, tell the story of your lives to the only one who understands! Quoting another priest, Hume calls the telling of this story *judgment*: "'Judgment is whispering into the ear of a merciful and compassionate God the story of my life which I had never been able to tell'".[151] Hume elaborates on the telling of our story:

> We each have a story, or part of one at any rate, about which we have never been able to speak to anyone. Fear of being misunderstood. Inability to understand. Ignorance of the darker side of our hidden lives, or even shame, make it very difficult for many people. Our true story is not told, or, only half of it is. What a relief it will be to whisper freely and fully into the merciful and compassionate ear of God. That is what God has always wanted. He waits for us to come home. He receives us, His prodigal children, with a loving embrace. In that embrace we start to tell Him our story.[152]

So reassuring are Hume's words: '[God] knows the burdens we have carried, the struggle too, the reasons for our failure and our sins.'[153]

All have a choice, though, to be received by His hands. As the author of the Book of Sirach writes, 'Before man are life and death, whichever he chooses shall be given him' (Si 15:17). For those who choose death 'fear indeed. And rightly so if arrogance, pride, avarice, cruelty have reigned and are not forgiven, because we have not sorrowed. We can refuse to be lifted by those hands, remaining self-sufficient, steeped in evil and empty. Our judgment will be swift, for we stand self-condemned.'[154] Those who choose life are 'those who have not turned away, but in spite of failure, weakness, and sin have not rejected him, we shall approach, trembling, nervous, no doubt, but reassured and at peace'.[155] 'These are the people who have discovered, in the carrying of their cross, the secret of the Resurrection—that new life comes from the dying seed. They have made themselves one with Jesus Christ in his Passion and Death. They share with Him now that new life, the divine life, which was His when He rose from the dead, and first comes to us when we are baptized.'[156] Be assured: 'That divine life in us will grow, if we allow it, and it is often through pain and sorrow that this will happen.'[157] It is then that the Lord 'whispers into our ear, "Come." Then we enter, happy and ready to wait till purified and made worthy to be with Him and rest forever in those loving hands.'[158]

Father, into Thy hands I commend my spirit. 'Serene peaceful full of joy He gives Himself in His last breath back to the hands that first fashioned the earth's dust into man. They will take Him down and bury Him, but the tomb of death will not hold captive the giver of life. Not for Him the return to dust, but the triumph of the Resurrection.'[159] The Cross points to new life in the Resurrection so: 'Whoever is in Christ is a new creation: the old things have passed away; behold, new things have come' (2 Co 5:17). 'He made all things new, suffering and death as well, your suffering and your death, too.'[160] 'There is no Good Friday experience that does not lead to greater understanding of and sharing in the joys and triumphs of Easter Sunday. Resurrection can become for each of us a daily experience.'[161] Come what may, 'every slight pain, every small anxiety, misunderstandings, disappointments, and life's contradictions—all of these are experiences of little deaths. Our daily hurts, and every one of them, have within them the joy of resurrection.'[162]

Father, into Thy hands I commend my spirit. In the homily he preached at Hume's funeral, Bishop John Crowley, Hume's personal secretary of six years, related: 'In those last few days here on earth [Cardinal Hume] came to a fresh understanding of the Our Father. It was, he said, like discovering its inner meaning for the very first time.'[163] Hume, echoing Thomas Aquinas who called the Lord's Prayer the most perfect prayer,[164] remarked, "'It's only now that I begin to glimpse how everything we need is contained right there in the Lord's own prayer.'"[165] Crowley continued:

> In the presence of a friend he then prayed the opening three sentences of the Our Father, adding each time a tiny commentary of his own. To sit there with him and to listen to what he said was to understand afresh all that he stood for. It was to be the recipient again, in a wonderfully privileged way, of his most special gift. As few others have done he raised our minds and hearts right up into the presence of God.[166]

Father, into Thy hands I commend my spirit.

Our Father who art in heaven hallowed be Thy name:
to sing the praises of God,
it is that for which we were made,
and it is that which will be for all eternity,
our greatest joy.

Thy Kingdom come:
the Gospel values of Jesus—justice, love,
and peace—embraced throughout the whole world and
in all their fullness.

Thy will be done on earth as it is in heaven:
that is the only thing which really matters.
What God wants for us
is what is best for us.[167]

Father, into Thy hands I commend my spirit.

Hume as Witness

Shortly after learning of his impending death, Hume put into practice his own preaching and teaching on the Cross and the Last Words of Jesus in two ways. First, he went to pray before the crucifix,[168] whereby he modelled monastic theology, that is, theology on its knees: 'Look at the cross, venerate it, embrace it in your prayer.'[169] As related by John Crowley, 'When the doctors first told him of his advanced cancer, [Hume] went straight to the hospital chapel where he sat praying for half an hour.'[170] Hume remarked on that occasion, '"I had preached so often on the seven last words of Jesus from the Cross ... now it was wonderful to find they were such a part of me."' [171] So important is the crucifix for the one in search for God, Hume stated, 'Looking prayerfully at the image of Christ dying on the Cross is an essential exercise for all who are in search of God.'[172] Prayer in front of the crucifix was important for Hume; it provided solace at times when words and even thoughts do not come easily—times when 'It is helpful then just to sit or kneel, gazing at the crucifix. That is an excellent way of praying.'[173] Hume himself experienced such times in the days leading to his death. As noted by biographer Anthony Howard, Hume began a custom in the early phases of his illness, when 'he could no longer either read or pray and had to be content with simply holding the crucifix and reflecting on Christ's suffering.'[174] Hume continued the practice in hospital when 'For the most part, in these last days he said his prayers through a sense of touch, keeping a crucifix in his hand and feeling Christ's wounds with his fingers.'[175]

Hume found prayer in front of the crucifix helpful when facing his own physical decline. In an address to senior citizens, himself included, he said, 'our energy and our strength today is not what it was yesterday. There are problems and there are aches and pains which we did not know in the afternoon of our lives.'[176] Hume stressed, 'it is only by looking at Christ crucified on the Cross that we can ever make sense of what befalls us.'[177] On another occasion, Hume told the priests of the archdiocese that the only solution to the problems of suffering and evil encountered in pastoral care was in looking at the crucifix: 'there, and there alone is the solution because behind every crucifix you see, with the eyes of faith, the outline of the risen Christ.'[178] Hume called the 'crucified Christ' a 'book', a book that must be studied to answer why there is so much evil in the world.[179] With the eyes of faith, Hume sought to understand his own death through the lens of the crucified Christ. Hume believed: 'Behind every crucifix, hidden, for we cannot see him, stands our Risen Lord. Hidden in every suffering and pain is the joy of closer union with him. His is the victory. He invites us to share it.'[180] In making the crucifix part of prayer, suffering, pain, and death are raised to a higher level, they 'have now a special dignity and value precisely because Christ, who is God, experienced them.'[181] Here one recalls the Letter to the Hebrews: 'Because [Christ] Himself was tested through what He suffered, He is able to help those who are being tested' (Heb 2:18). In the crucifix, then, 'Slowly we see, and then only dimly, that in suffering of all kinds there is new life to be found, and therefore hope. It would have not been so if Christ had not risen from the dead.'[182] As Hume noted, 'you only learn the secret of the Resurrection when you have learnt the secret of the Cross.'[183]

The second way in which Hume practised his preaching and teaching occurred three days after his diagnosis. Hume wrote a letter to the priests of Westminster in which he shared the reception of two graces that would enable him to live out his faith: 'I have received two wonderful graces. First, I have been given time to prepare for a new future. Secondly, I find myself—uncharacteristically—calm and at peace.'[184] Hume surrendered both mind and heart, he was calm, at peace; qualities affirmed by Chief Rabbi Jonathan Sacks who described Hume as 'serene in life, serene in the face of death'.[185] Hume's life was one of preparation. He knew, as he said on one occasion: 'This life is a period of training, a time of preparation, during which we learn the art of loving God and our neighbour, the heart of the Gospel message, sometimes succeeding, sometimes failing.'[186] While accepting his limitations, Hume's journey of training and preparation was not over as he told the priests, 'I intend to carry on working as much and as long as I can. I have no intention of being an invalid until I have to submit to the illness. But nevertheless, I shall be a bit limited in what I can do.'[187] More than anything though, Hume wanted 'no fuss'.[188] He intended to keep going, and encouraged the priests to do likewise by continuing to learn the art of charity, that is, the heart of the Gospel message. Emphatically, he stated, 'The Gospel must live again in our society.'[189] By receiving and sharing the Gospel message of Christ's love, believers, with fellow pilgrim Cardinal Hume, move 'through life like pilgrims heading towards our final destination … when we shall find total fulfilment',[190] which 'must consist in an experience of love because love is the highest of all human experience. To love totally, to be loved completely. It is in union with that which is most lovable that we become fully ourselves.'[191] Life and death, then, become an encounter of love meeting love. In this, Hume was exemplar.

Hume, ever the realist, taught, 'The Christian faces death realistically, but also knows that death is a gateway, a new beginning, a fulfilment of human life.'[192] Even so, Hume, fully human, questioned death while in hospital, 'exclaiming: "Why doesn't God take me?" or "Why is He keeping me waiting?"'[193] Speaking after the death of Diana, Princess of Wales, Hume said, 'Death is a formidable foe until we learn to make it a friend.'[194] Making death our friend is our faith, as 'faith is the realization of what is hoped for and evidence of things not seen' (Heb 11:1). Hume continued, 'Death is the ultimate absurdity if we do not see it as fulfilment. Death haunts us when viewed as a journey into nothingness rather than a pilgrimage to a place where true happiness is to be found.'[195] On another occasion while using different words, Hume said: 'Life is indeed meaningless and absurd if its only future is nothingness.'[196] Some of Hume's most profound words on life and death are found in a 'series of brief meditations on death, and life after death,'[197] shared at a Requiem Mass:

First thoughts about death are normally ones of fear and dread. It is partly having to face the unknown, partly recoiling from the final agony as we lie helpless and perhaps wired up to all those machines competing for access to our body. Some thoughts tell us there is no future, only a blank nothing, we are no more. Another thought comes and tells us how quickly we are forgotten. In a very bad moment, I think about the relief my death will bring to some people. I worry about the insensitive and clumsy ways I have handled some people.

But there is another voice that speaks within us. It is not a voice that depresses and frightens. It has a very different message. You have loved so many people in your life; are you to be frustrated and denied that love which you have sought throughout your life? It is not so.

This is an instinct which speaks of hope leading to life after death. In the animal world, the instinct for survival is strong. It is so with humans as well. We want to go on, unless overwhelmed by depression or weariness. Our fear is that we may not. That instinct beckons us. Our mind says, 'It may be. It must be.' Then faith finally takes over and triumphantly declares 'It is so'. The instinct for survival is a true one. It does not deceive. How could it be otherwise since it is God given? Faith brings the reassurance which instinct was seeking.[198]

The news of Cardinal Hume's imminent death had a far-reaching impact. As noted by his nephew William Charles, 'When Father Basil's terminal illness became publicly known, he received, in the few short weeks before he died, some 5,000 letters. They came from a wide range of people and from many different corners of the world. Many referred to his books and the impact they had had on the writers.'[199] As evidenced by his influence on so many, Cardinal Hume is presented as a living *witness* of his preaching and teaching, a man who embodied *witness*, described by Pope Paul VI: 'Modern man listens more readily to witnesses than to teachers, and if he does listen to teachers, it is because they are

witnesses.'[200] As witness, Hume fulfilled his vocation as baptized
Christian, monk, priest, abbot, bishop and cardinal. Inspired by
Pope Paul's VI's encouragement to 'always remain a monk',[201]
Hume kept death daily before his eyes.[202] He knew the importance of reflecting on his own death, as he once said, 'It helps
me to look at the way I am living. It enables me to get a better
perspective.'[203] As monk, Hume yearned 'for everlasting life with
holy desire',[204] thereby encouraging the faithful not to fear death,
but to 'Welcome it when it comes. It is now a holy thing, made
so by Him who died that we might live.'[205] Returning again to
Hume's reflections on life and death: 'I now have no fear of death.
I look forward to this friend leading me to a world where I shall
know God and be known by Him as His beloved son.'[206]

Hume also continued to embrace the qualities of an abbot
as described by St Benedict, qualities important for any leader:
'Anyone who receives the name of abbot is to lead his disciples by
a twofold teaching: he must point out to them all that is good and
holy more by example than by words.'[207] The way in which Hume
accepted his death solidified his unique contribution to spirituality, a gift which enabled him not only to teach and preach the faith
in words accessible to all, but to model by his actions. Hume's life
and death were the 'spiritual notebook of a pilgrim',[208] a phrase
he used to describe one of his published works. In accepting
his own mortality, Hume revealed a spirituality of suffering, the
Cross, Death, and Resurrection. In both his immediate actions
and in the letter written to the priests of the Westminster archdiocese, he explicitly expressed his faith, a faith he described as
'the surrendering of our minds'[209] and 'the surrendering of our
hearts.'[210] Furthermore, 'Faith is an encounter with a person. It
is love meeting love.'[211]

In two final acts of grace, Hume, true to his word in the letter he
wrote to the priests of the diocese when he learned of his imminent death, Hume kept going until the end. Both acts occurred
during what Anthony Howard called Hume's 'last journey',[212]
just 15 days before he died. First, Hume left hospital for a visit to

Buckingham Palace where he received the Order of Merit from the Queen. In this mutual act of respect, the relationship established between Cardinal Hume and the Queen was solidified. Second, Hume insisted that he stop at Archbishop's House on his way to the Queen in order to express his gratitude and show respect to his staff. In the end, he dropped in 'at Archbishop's House both on the way out (in order to change) and then also on the way back (to say his goodbyes).'[213]

It is worth noting here Archbishop Arthur Roche's moving account of Hume's visit to the Queen:

> Then when he got to Buckingham Palace, the Queen had agreed to see him in a lower chamber, not in one of the state rooms which are above. And so she came down. And they brought out a wheelchair for him. And he said, 'What's that?' 'It's a wheelchair to take you into the Queen.' And he said, 'I will not go into my Sovereign sitting down.' Even those comments, many of the comments that he would make, really sort of opened up for you a view of the man, his sense of respect, his dignity. He went in and sat down, the Queen was there. And she said to him, 'What is it like?' 'Well, Mam, it's rather like sitting in a theatre, a darkened theatre before the curtain is opened, and you can't see beyond the curtain but you know that something is there waiting for you. That is what it is like at this present moment. I am waiting for the curtains to be drawn back to see Christ.' [214]

Always the monk, always embracing the qualities of the abbot, ever the pilgrim, Basil Hume remained witness in both life and death. He related to people. He accepted them wherever they were, and strove to walk with them on their pilgrim journey. Hume's personal secretary shared an example of Hume's gift of relating to and accepting others. In a letter Hume received after announcing his illness, the writer revealed strong emotions:

> You have accepted your illness and are at peace ... I learned I was terminally ill the same day as you made that

announcement. I am far from happy—I am frightened and
I am angry and I am especially angry with you because
everyone will pray for you—but no one will pray for
me—a lapsed Catholic who is divorced ...[215]

Sharing the writer's burdens, sharing the writer's cross, Hume
promptly replied: "'Don't ever say no one will pray for you for
from this day on I will pray for you every day'".[216] In haste, the
writer responded: "'I was so ashamed when I read your gener-
ous letter ... I was angry and bitter, forgive me'".[217] With mutual
compassion, in shared mutual experiences, Hume and the writer
encountered the living and true God, grew closer to one another,
and shared in Christ's work of redemption.

In a 1971 abbatial conference, Hume gave warning: 'There is
a danger of constructing a spirituality which will not face up to
the Cross as a predominant element.'[218] By nature, we fear death.
Like the apostles who listened to Jesus predict His Passion on
three occasions, we do not understand the Cross. However, as
Hume made clear, 'we need to remind ourselves again and again
that the Cross is, and must be, an element in a life in which we
truly follow Christ. And it is only in the intimacy of private prayer
that we will do this, and learn to do it.'[219] Over and over again,
Hume embraced the Cross in prayer. In life and death, Hume
articulated a Christian truth: 'rejoice to the extent that you share
in the sufferings of Christ, so that when His glory is revealed you
may also rejoice exultantly' (1 Pt 4:13), a truth echoed by St Benedict: 'We shall through patience share in the sufferings of Christ
that we may also deserve to share in His Kingdom.'[220] Hume
well summarized this truth in the words of that 1971 conference:

> The wish that should constantly be ours is to share whatever
> Christ wants of us; to fear nothing; to be detached as far
> as we can; to prefer nothing, as St Benedict says, to the
> love of Christ and therefore to want nothing other than
> what He wants us to accept and endure for His sake; to be
> firmly convinced that if we learn to do this we will attain a

true understanding of Christ's mission to the world, and ourselves share in His redeeming work. Only through following him as Redeemer shall we be able to share in His Resurrection and, ultimately, in that glory of His when He, the Son of Man, will appear on the last day.[221]

Reflection

Hume's teaching and preaching presented the foundation by which one can call Hume a *witness* as described by Pope Paul VI and by St Benedict too when he exhorts the monk 'to day by day remind yourself that you are going to die',[222] and when he describes the abbot as one who teaches by the example of the life he leads.[223] Hume's teaching and preaching were modelled by his acceptance of his own death and subsequent actions. Hume taught and preached as witness making his influence strong and far reaching. Hume, like St Benedict, was in touch with the human condition.[224] As witness, Hume put his listeners in touch with the living and true God whom he not only loved, but liked as an intimate friend. Hume was witness, a kind of herald about whom John Paul II spoke: 'We need heralds of the Gospel who are experts in humanity, who know the depths of the human heart, who can share the joys, the hopes, the agonies, the distress of people today, but who are, at the same time, contemplatives who have fallen in love with God.'[225] It was noted that Cardinal Hume often said, '"Never forget, we are dealing with people first of all, not principles."'[226] Speaking after Hume's death, Jonathan Sacks said of Hume, 'When I think of Cardinal Hume, I recall the words of Judaism's early sages. They asked: "Who is a hero?" They answered: "One who turns strangers into friends." That was his great gift. He drew people to him by his love of God and his deep feeling for humanity. While you were with him you felt enlarged. He was a friend, and we were lucky to have him.'[227]

Hume's spirituality of the Cross and his presence as witness and herald is well summarized in the epilogue to his published meditations on Jesus' Seven Last Words. There, one will find 'how important to him was the crucifix in his chapel in the archbishop's house:'[228]

> I like that because sometimes in the morning when you're tired and have a lot of worries in your head, it's not easy to get the head up to God, so you have to pray with your eyes. Sometimes I just sit and look at the cross and say to myself: in all hospitals there are people dying. A lot of people I meet or who write letters to me are suffering terribly at this moment. So, looking at the cross, I think of all those people sharing that passion, sharing the agony of the Lord. And if God became man—as indeed He did—He came to share a lot of what we all have to live and undergo and gives it meaning and purpose and makes it holy. I find that very powerful, and when people say to me, 'I'm very worried' or 'I've just lost my husband' or 'There's been a terrible tragedy in our family—please pray for me,' I say, 'Yes, I'll do it tomorrow morning.' So sitting in the chapel, looking at the crucifix, I remember that person.[229]

NOTES

[1]   B. Hume, *Searching for God* (New York: Paulist Press, 1978), p. 142.

[2]   B. Hume, unpublished conference, 12 May 1965, used with permission of the Ampleforth Abbey Trust, York.

[3]   *Ibid.*

[4]   Hume, *Searching for God*, p. 142.

[5]   *Ibid.*

[6]   *Ibid.*

[7]   *Ibid.*

[8]   Hume, unpublished conference, 27 January 1967.

[9]   *RB* 49:2–3.

[10]   Hume, unpublished conference, 8 February 1967.

[11]   Hume, unpublished conference, 27 January 1967.

12 *Ibid.*

13 Hume, unpublished conference, 8 February 1967.

14 *Ibid.*

15 *Ibid.*

16 *Ibid.*

17 *Ibid.*

18 Hume, unpublished conference, 27 May 1975.

19 Hume, unpublished conference, 8 February 1967.

20 *Ibid.*

21 B. Hume, *The Mystery of the Cross*, 2nd ed. (Brewster, MA: Paraclete Press, 2000), p. 12.

22 *Ibid.*, p. 3.

23 Hume, unpublished conference, 8 February 1967.

24 *Ibid.*

25 *Ibid.*

26 Hume, unpublished conference, 27 May 1975.

27 *Ibid.*

28 *Ibid.*

29 Hume, unpublished conference, 8 February 1967.

30 *Ibid.*

31 Hume, unpublished conference, 27 January 1967.

32 Hume, unpublished conference, 27 May 1975.

33 *Ibid.*

34 Vatican II, Pastoral Constitution *Gaudium et Spes*, 22.

35 Hume, unpublished conference, 27 May 1975.

36 Hume, unpublished conference, 8 February 1967.

37 *Ibid.*

38 *Ibid.*

39 *Ibid.*

40 Hume, unpublished conference, 8 February 1967.

41 *Gaudium et Spes*, 22.

42 Hume, *Searching for God*, p. 154.

43 Hume, unpublished conference, 27 May 1975.

44 'Review', in *Ampleforth Journal*, vol. 68/issue 2 (1963), p. 178.

45 L. Kelly in B. Hume, *Hope from the Cross: Reflections on Jesus' Seven Last Words*, ed. L. Kelly (repr. Ijamsville, MD: Word Among Us Press, 2010), pp. 10–11.

46 Hume, *Hope from the Cross*, p. 16.

47 B. Hume, unpublished meditations on *The Seven Last Words of Christ on the Cross*, 10 March 1963, used with permission of the Ampleforth Abbey Trust, York.

48 Hume, *Hope from the Cross*, p. 18.

49 *Ibid.*

50 *Ibid.*

51 Hume, unpublished meditations.

52 Hume, *Hope from the Cross*, pp. 18–19.

53 *Ibid.*, 19.

54 *Ibid.*, 23.

55 *Ibid.*, 20.

56 *Ibid.*, p. 23.

57 *Ibid.*, p. 20.

58 Hume, unpublished meditations.

59 *Ibid.*

60 Hume, *Hope from the Cross*, p. 20.

61 *Ibid.*, p. 24.

62 *Ibid.*

63 *Ibid.*

64 Hume, unpublished meditations.

65 Hume, *Hope from the Cross*, p. 26.

66 *Ibid.*

67 *Ibid.*

68 *Ibid.*, p. 30.

69 Hume, unpublished meditations.

70 Hume, *Hope from the Cross*, p. 30.

71 *Ibid.*, p. 29.

72 *Ibid.*

73 Hume, unpublished meditations.

74 *Ibid.*

75 Hume, *Hope from the Cross*, p. 30.

76 Hume, unpublished meditations.

77 Hume, *Hope from the Cross*, p. 30.

78 RB 4:26.

79 RB 4:18–19.

80 Hume, *Hope from the Cross*, p. 31.

81 *Ibid.*, p. 32.

82 Hume, unpublished meditations.

83 'The Communion Rite', in *The Roman Missal*, English Translation According to the Third Typical Edition (New Jersey: Catholic Book Publishing, 2011), p. 521.
84 Hume, *Hope from the Cross*, p. 28.
85 *RB* Prologue 38.
86 Hume, *Hope from the Cross*, p. 32.
87 *Ibid.*
88 *Ibid.*, pp. 28–9.
89 Hume, unpublished meditations.
90 *Ibid.*
91 Hume, *The Mystery of the Cross*, p. 17.
92 Hume, unpublished meditations.
93 Hume, *Hope from the Cross*, p. 36.
94 *Ibid.*, p. 38–9.
95 *Ibid.*, p. 39.
96 *Ibid.*, p. 40.
97 *Ibid.*
98 Hume, unpublished meditations.
99 *Ibid.*
100 *Ibid.*
101 Hume, *Hope from the Cross*, p. 44.
102 *Ibid.*, p. 42.
103 *Ibid.*, pp. 44–5.
104 *Ibid.*, p. 42.
105 Hume, unpublished meditations.
106 Hume, *Hope from the Cross*, p. 44.
107 *Ibid.*, p. 47.
108 *Ibid.*, pp. 42–3.
109 *Ibid.*, p. 43.
110 *Ibid.*, pp. 46–7.
111 Hume, unpublished meditations.
112 *Ibid.*
113 Hume, *Hope from the Cross*, p. 51.
114 *Ibid.*, p. 55.
115 *Ibid.*
116 *Ibid.*, p. 51.
117 *Ibid.*
118 *Ibid.*, p. 52.

[119] *Ibid.*

[120] *Ibid.*, pp. 52–3.

[121] *Ibid.*, p. 53.

[122] Hume, unpublished meditations.

[123] *Ibid.*

[124] Hume, *Hope from the Cross*, p. 54.

[125] *Ibid.*, p. 56.

[126] *Ibid.*, p. 55.

[127] *Ibid.*, p. 56.

[128] *Ibid.*, p. 53.

[129] *Ibid.*

[130] Hume, unpublished meditations.

[131] Hume, *Hope from the Cross*, p. 58.

[132] *Ibid.*, p. 61.

[133] Hume, unpublished meditations.

[134] Hume, *Hope from the Cross*, p. 64.

[135] Hume, *The Mystery of the Cross*, pp. 81–2.

[136] Hume, *Hope from the Cross*, pp. 62–3.

[137] *Ibid.*, p. 63.

[138] Hume, unpublished meditations.

[139] Hume, *Hope from the Cross*, p. 61.

[140] Hume, unpublished meditations.

[141] Hume, *Hope from the Cross*, p. 63.

[142] Hume, unpublished meditations.

[143] Hume, *Hope from the Cross*, pp. 63–4.

[144] *Ibid.*, p. 64.

[145] *Ibid.*, pp. 64–5.

[146] *Ibid.*, p. 61.

[147] Hume, unpublished meditations.

[148] Hume, *Hope from the Cross*, pp. 69–70.

[149] *Ibid.*, p. 72.

[150] *Ibid.*, pp. 72–3.

[151] Anonymous priest in Hume, *To Be a Pilgrim: A Spiritual Notebook* (repr. London: SPCK Classics, 2009), p. 228.

[152] B. Hume in G. Stack, 'Homily at a Requiem Mass' Westminster Cathedral, 18 June 1999 in P. Walesby and M. Webster, eds., *Homilies Given at the Funeral Rites of Cardinal George Basil Hume, OSB, OM* (London: Abbeyville Printing, n.d.), p. 10.

153 Hume, *Hope from the Cross*, p. 74.

154 *Ibid.*, pp. 73–4.

155 *Ibid.*, p. 74.

156 *Ibid.*, p. 70.

157 *Ibid.*

158 *Ibid.*, p. 75.

159 Hume, unpublished meditations.

160 Hume, *Hope from the Cross*, p. 71.

161 *Ibid.*, p. 70.

162 *Ibid.*

163 J. Crowley in W. Charles, ed., *Basil Hume: Ten Years On* (London: Burns & Oates, 2009), p. 203.

164 St Thomas Aquinas, *Summa Theologica*, II-II, q. 83, art. 9.

165 Hume in Charles, ed., *Basil Hume: Ten Years On*, p. 203.

166 Crowley in Charles, ed., *Basil Hume: Ten Years On*, p. 203.

167 Hume as related by J. Crowley in B. Hume, *The Mystery of Love* (repr. Brewster, MA: Paraclete Press, 2001), p. ix. In an email correspondence of 6 March 2015, Bishop Crowley responded to the question: 'Did Cardinal Hume only comment on the first three sentences of the Our Father?' Crowley wrote, 'My memory tells me that it was just on those first three sentences of the Our Father that Cardinal Hume shared those thoughts with me so movingly on his death bed. All that he spoke of on that occasion is related in his funeral homily.'

168 L. Kelly in Hume, *Hope from the Cross*, p. 9.

169 Hume, *The Mystery of the Cross*, p. 15.

170 J. Crowley, 'Epilogue', in Charles, ed. *Basil Hume: Ten Years On*, p. 202.

171 Hume as related by Crowley, 'Epilogue', in Charles, ed. *Basil Hume: Ten Years On*, pp. 202–203.

172 Hume, *The Mystery of the Cross*, p. vii.

173 *Ibid.*, p. 17.

174 A. Howard, *Basil Hume: The Monk Cardinal* (London: Headline, 2005), p. 310.

175 *Ibid.*

176 Hume, *To Be a Pilgrim*, p. 226.

177 *Ibid.*

178 B. Hume, *Light in the Lord: Reflections on the Priesthood* (repr. Collegeville: Liturgical Press, 1993) p. 134.

179 Hume, *The Mystery of the Cross*, p. 28.

180 Hume, *The Mystery of Love*, p. 69.

181 Hume, *The Mystery of the Cross*, p. 18.

[182] *Ibid.*, p. 28.

[183] Hume, unpublished conference, 1 April 1966.

[184] B. Hume, Letter to the Priests of the Archdiocese of Westminster, 16 April 1999. Letter sent via email by L. Kelly, 14 January 2015. Used with permission of the Ampleforth Abbey Trust.

[185] J. Sacks, 'Turning Strangers into Friends', in *Catholic Herald* (25 June 1999), p. 7.

[186] Hume, *To Be a Pilgrim*, p. 230.

[187] Hume, 'Letter to the Priests of the Archdiocese of Westminster.'

[188] *Ibid.*

[189] *Ibid.*

[190] Hume, *To Be a Pilgrim*, p. 228.

[191] *Ibid.*

[192] *Ibid.*, p. 227.

[193] Hume in Howard, *Basil Hume: The Monk Cardinal*, p. 310.

[194] Hume, *The Mystery of the Cross*, p. 73.

[195] *Ibid.*, p. 74.

[196] *Ibid.*, p. 24.

[197] G. Stack, 'Homily at a Requiem Mass', pp. 9–10.

[198] B. Hume quoted in Stack, 'Homily at a Requiem Mass,' pp. 9–10.

[199] Charles, ed. *Basil Hume: Ten Years On*, p. 132.

[200] Pope Paul VI, *Address to the Members of the Consilium de Laicis* (2 October 1974) quoted in Pope Paul VI, Apostolic Exhortation *Evangelii Nuntiandi*, 41.

[201] Pope Paul VI in A. Howard, *Basil Hume: The Monk Cardinal*, p. 97. Cardinal Cormac Murphy-O'Connor commented on a meeting in 1976 between Hume and Paul VI, shortly after Hume was appointed Archbishop of Westminster. The Pope said to Hume, 'Keep your Benedictine spirit.' C. Murphy-O'Connor, interview by author, Venerable English College, Rome, Italy, 29 November 2013.

[202] See *RB* 4:47.

[203] Hume, *To Be a Pilgrim*, p. 227.

[204] *RB* 4:46.

[205] Hume, *To Be a Pilgrim*, p. 228.

[206] Hume quoted in Stack, 'Homily at a Requiem Mass,' p. 10.

[207] *RB* 2:11–12.

[208] Hume, *To Be a Pilgrim*, p. 11.

[209] B. Hume, *The Mystery of the Incarnation* (repr. Brewster, MA: Paraclete Press, 2000), p. 21.

[210] *Ibid.*

[211] *Ibid.*

[212] Howard, *Basil Hume: The Monk Cardinal*, p. 307.

[213] *Ibid.*

[214] A. Roche, interview by author, Rome, Italy, 26 November 2013. When he served as General Secretary of the Catholic Bishops' Conference of England and Wales, Roche wrote the summary text of Cardinal Hume's life which was placed in the Cardinal's coffin on the day of his burial. See Appendix.

[215] Anonymous letter writer quoted by S. McAllister, 'Colleague and Friend', in Charles, ed., *Basil Hume: Ten Years On*, pp. 107–108.

[216] Hume quoted by McAllister, 'Colleague and Friend,' p. 108.

[217] Anonymous letter writer quoted by McAllister, 'Colleague and Friend,' p. 108.

[218] Hume, *Searching for God*, p. 149.

[219] *Ibid.*

[220] *RB* Prologue 50.

[221] Hume, *Searching for God*, p. 149.

[222] *RB* 4:47.

[223] See *RB* 2:12.

[224] Pope Benedict XVI said of St Benedict: 'The great monk [Benedict] is still a true master at whose school we can learn to become proficient in true humanism.' Pope Benedict XVI, *General Audience on St Benedict of Nursia: The Great Monk is Still a True Teacher* (9 April 2008).

[225] Pope St John Paul II, *Speech at the 6th Symposium of the Council of the Episcopal Conferences of Europe (CCEE)* (11 October 1985). English translation, Hume, *The Mystery of Love*, p. iii.

[226] Hume by Kelly 'Introduction', in B. Hume, *Cardinal Hume: A Spiritual Companion*, 2nd ed. (Brewster, MA: Paraclete Press, 2001) p. 7.

[227] Sacks, 'Turning Strangers into Friends', p. 7.

[228] L. Kelly in Hume, *Hope from the Cross*, p. 77.

[229] Hume, *Hope from the Cross*, pp. 77–8.

Conclusion

Basil Hume's Benedictine spirituality was the inspiration not only for the conferences he gave to his monks, but also for all the work he did for the wider Church. Significantly, on the 1500th anniversary of the birth of St Benedict, Hume remarked: 'St Benedict gathered ordinary people around him. Men and women came together in community and followed his Rule in their own monasteries as they still do today. He gave them a new way of looking at life, precisely because they were to learn to put God at the very centre of their lives. That is the key for all of us.'[1]

Basil Hume was a man of great sincerity, a humble man endowed with a spirit of life and a quality of faith so simple and yet so profound it enabled him to speak with authority. Hume's early formation in the family, what he called 'the school in which we learn the art of living',[2] provided an environment that equipped him to grow into a man of spiritual maturity during his years as student, monk, teacher, and Abbot of Ampleforth Abbey. His dedication to a stable life of prayer and work at Ampleforth was the firm foundation upon which he stood. A man in love with Christ, Hume was well prepared to be the spiritual leader of the people of England and Wales.

As abbot, Hume offers an approach to Benedictine spirituality that is distinctively his own. With vision and clarity of thought, Basil Hume articulates an authentic Benedictine life based solely on a Rule which has endured for over 1,500 years. To Benedictines gathered at Westminster Cathedral, Hume said: 'Monasteries

throughout the centuries have come into being and then dis-
appeared again—either destroyed from without by enemies,
or disintegrated from within from lack of zeal and good observance—but the Rule remained.'³ Initially in the environment of
the novitiate, the Benedictine learns 'the raison d'être of every
monastic vocation is "to seek God"'.⁴ Throughout the monastic
life the Benedictine develops the art of searching for God, or
in other words: 'The art of being a Christian and therefore the
art of being a monk is to learn to put God at the centre—the
love of God and of our neighbour; to be devoted to God and to
our neighbour.'⁵ Charity, then, is the theological implication of
the life-long search for God: 'our respect for one another, our
tolerance. We should always be ready to admire each other, to
hold each other in respect; to feel, too, deep concern and deep
compassion. After all, our search for God is our response to a love
which He has first shown to us. And so we can learn from one
another and together, as a community, return to Him.'⁶ After all,
'there is only one spirituality, there is only one Christianity, there
is only one supreme law, and it is the law of charity.'⁷

During his years as Archbishop, Hume was a pastor of prayer
seeing with the eyes of Christ. His principal message was the relationship between the search for God and prayer presented as a
spiritual pilgrimage, articulated by Hume in the following words:

> To go in search of God … requires effort, and a measure of
> self-discipline and self-denial. The voice of God does not
> speak dramatically, as in a hurricane or an earthquake or a
> fire but calls to us gently in the very depths of our being. To
> hear the voice of God demands some solitude, silence, and
> stillness. In our society today there is too much noise, both
> around and within us, and the quiet voice of God becomes
> stifled. But in a moment of gentle stillness, God not only
> reveals something of Himself but He transforms us too.
> For if God exists, it is the most fundamental truth of all.
> It changes everything. It cannot be true and not matter.⁸

Inspired by the English saints of Northumbria, Hume learned
to be a shepherd and gifted communicator who could relate to
others who joined him on the spiritual pilgrimage. Hume looked
for Christ in others, especially the sick and suffering, and those
victims of injustice. Hume also took great care in being of service
to the priests in his archdiocese, what he considered to be his
first responsibility.

Basil Hume was a teacher and preacher of the Cross, focusing
primarily on Suffering, the Cross, Death, and Resurrection. As
such, Hume, the monk and Archbishop, meditated frequently
on the Last Words of Jesus. Finally, Basil Hume was *witness* of
his teaching and preaching as he modelled by the acceptance of
his own death.

The voice of Basil Hume continues to speak to all those who
are searching for meaning and purpose in a loud, busy, and vio-
lent world. Yearning was the core of Basil Hume's search for God
and yearning is the core of all those who seek God, whether they
know it or not, best stated by Hume himself: 'We are made in
the image and likeness of God and there is in each of us a yearning—consciously recognized or not—for the Father and source
of our being.'[9]

NOTES

[1]   B. Hume, *In Praise of Benedict 480–1980 A.D.* (Petersham, MA: Saint Bede's
Publications, 1981), pp. 85–6.

[2]   B. Hume, *Remaking Europe: The Gospel in a Divided Continent* (London:
SPCK, 1994), p. 33.

[3]   Hume, *In Praise of Benedict*, pp. 57–8.

[4]   B. Hume, *To Be a Pilgrim: A Spiritual Notebook* (repr. London: SPCK
Classics, 2009), p. 38.

[5]   B. Hume, *Searching for God* (New York: Paulist Press, 1978), p. 39.

[6]   *Ibid.*, p. 89.

[7]   B. Hume, unpublished conference, 20 March 1967, used with permission
of the Ampleforth Abbey Trust, York.

[8]   Hume, *Remaking Europe*, p. 25.

[9]   B. Hume, *Towards a Civilization of Love: Being Church in Today's World*
(London: Hodder & Stoughton, 1995), p. 96.

Appendix

This summary text of Cardinal Hume's life, written by Mgr A. Roche, General Secretary of the Catholic Bishops' Conference of England and Wales, is the official record of the Cardinal's life. It was placed in his coffin on the day of his burial; his coffin lies in the Chapel of St Gregory and St Augustine, in Westminster Cathedral. This is the *Rogito* encased in his tomb.

Orate pro me

Georgio Basilio Hume, OSB

Hic iacet corpus Eminentiae Suae Georgii Basilii Hume, O.S.B., O.M., Sanctae Romanae Ecclesiae Cardinalis Presbyteri, titulo Sancti Silvestri in Capite, Archiepiscopi Westmonasteriensis noni, et Praesidis Conferentiae Episcoporum Angliae et Cambriae.

Primi Anni

Georgius Hume natus est die 2 mensis Martii anno 1923 in civitate Newcastle upon Tyne, filius natu maximus Equitis Gulielmi et Dominae Hume (nata Tysseyre); pater medicus consultor fuit, bene notus; mater, gentis Gallicae, Catholica erat.

Educatio

Educatus est in Collegio Ampleforth in comitatu Yorkshire; deinde in Aula Sancti Benedicti in Universitate Oxoniense, ubi Historiae studebat; postea Theologiae studium secutus est in Universitate Friburgii in Helvetia.

Monachus et Abbas

Anno 1941 monasterium Benedictinum Sancti Laurentii apud Ampleforth in comitatu Yorkshire intravit, assumens nomen religiosum Basilium. Professione simplice monastica anno 1942 facta, vota solemnia fecit anno 1945. Sacerdos ordinatus est apud Ampleforth die 23 Iulii anno 1950. Post ordinationem officia in monasterio assumpsit quae sequuntur: Magister Senior Linguarum Hodiernarum; Magister Domus Sancti Bedae; Professor

Appendix

The English translation presented here in parallel to the Latin text is taken from P. Walesby and M. Webster, eds., *Homilies given at the Funeral Rites of Cardinal George Basil Hume, OSB, OM* (London: Abbeyville Printing, n.d.), pp. 5–8.

Pray for me
George Basil Hume, OSB

Here lie the remains of His Eminence George Basil Cardinal Hume, OSB, OM, Cardinal Priest of the Holy Roman Church of the title of San Silvestro in Capite, ninth Archbishop of Westminster and President of the Bishops' Conference of England and Wales.

Early Years

George Hume was born on 2 March 1923 in Newcastle upon Tyne, the eldest son of Sir William and Lady Hume (née Tysseyre). His father was a well known consultant physician. His mother was French and a Catholic.

Education

Educated at Ampleforth College in Yorkshire, and later at St Benet's Hall, Oxford, where he read History, and at Fribourg University Switzerland, where he studied Theology.

Monk and Abbot

He entered the Benedictine Monastery of St Laurence, Ampleforth, Yorkshire, in 1941, taking the religious name of Basil. He was simply professed as a monk in 1942 and took solemn vows in 1945. He was ordained a priest at Ampleforth on 23 July 1950. After ordination he held the following appointments in the Abbey: Senior Master in Modern Languages; Housemaster of St Bede's; Professor of Dogmatic Theology; Magister Scholarum of the

Theologiae Dogmaticae; Magister Scholarum Congregationis Benedictinae Anglicae; instruebat etiam in Collegio ludores "Quindecim" vocatos in ludo "Rugby" nomine. Abbas monasterii apud Ampleforth electus est die 17 Aprilis anno 1963. Usque ad annum 1976 ducebat 150 monachos, quorum labor pastoralis comprehendebat non tantum scholam sed etiam operam pastoralem in Anglia Septentrionali et in Cambria. Anno 1971 iterum Abbas electus est pro altera periodo.

Electus Episcopus et Cardinalis
Die 17 mensis Februarii anno 1976 a Papa Paulo VI electus est, ut successor Ioannis Carmeli Cardinalis Heenan, Archiepiscopus Westmonasteriensis. Consecratus et inauguratus est Episcopus die 25 Martii anno 1976, et die 24 Maii 1976 creatus Sanctae Romanae Eccesiae Cardinalis titulo Sancti Silvestri in Capite, in Consistorio illo die facto. Anno 1979 electus est Praeses Conferentiae Episcoporum Angliae et Cambriae, officium quod usque ad obitum tenebat; Praeses erat etiam Consilii Conferentiarum Episcopalium Europae; Relatoris munus implevit anno 1994 in Synodo Generali De Vita Consecrata; Praeses erat Operum Ecumenicorum: Consilium Ecclesiarum in Britannia et Hibernia atque Ecclesiae Coniunctae in Anglia; Praeses etiam Consilii Christianorum et Iudaeorum. Sequuntur nomina Congregationum quibus ut membrum serviebat: Congregatio pro Ecclesiis Orientalibus, Congregatio de Cultu Divino et Disciplina Sacramentorum; Congregatio pro Institutis Vitae Consecratae et Societatibus Vitae Apostolicae; Pontificium Consilium ad Unitatem Christianorum Fovendam; Pontificium Consilium de Apostolatu pro Valetudinis Administris.

Archiepiscopus Wesmonasteriensis Nonus
Consilium initiavit reformationis pastoralis dioeceseos suae, et quinque constituit Episcopos Regionales responsabiles quisque pro una Regionum Pastoralium dioeceseos. Debitum aerarium dioecesanum exstinxit; Scholam Cantorum Cathedralem salvavit ne clauderetur. Anni centesimi Ecclesiae Cathedralis celebrationi

English Benedictine Congregation; he also coached the School Rugby XV. He was appointed Abbot of Ampleforth on 17 April 1963. He led 150 monks whose pastoral work involved not only the school but also parish work in the north of England and Wales. He was re-elected abbot for a second term in 1971.

Appointment as Bishop and Cardinal

On 17 February 1976 he was appointed by Pope Paul VI to succeed John Carmel Cardinal Heenan as the ninth Archbishop of Westminster. He was consecrated and installed as Bishop on 25 March 1976, and created Cardinal Priest of the Holy Roman Church of the title of San Silvestro in Capite at the Consistory on 24 May 1976. In 1979 he was elected the President of the Bishops' Conference of England and Wales, a post which he held until his death. He was President of the European Council of Episcopal Conferences; acted as Relator at the 1994 General Synod on Consecrated Life; President of the ecumenical instruments, Churches Together in Britain in Ireland and Churches Together in England; President of the Council of Christians and Jews. He served as a member of the Congregation for Sacraments and Divine Worship; Congregation for Religious and Secular Institutes; Congregation for Eastern Churches; Pontifical Council for the Promotion of Christian Unity; and Pontifical Council for Pastoral Assistance to Health Care Workers.

Ninth Archbishop of Westminster

He began a plan of pastoral re-organisation of the diocese and established five Area Bishops, each with responsibility for one of the five Pastoral Areas of the Diocese. He eliminated the debt of the diocese and saved the Cathedral Choir School from closure. He presided over the centenary of the Cathedral in 1995, and in

praesidebat anno 1995; eodem anno prima vice post Reforma-
tionem ad celebrationem religiosam Catholicam recepit cum
gaudio Anglos regentem, Suam Maiestatem Reginam Elizabeth
II, quae Vesperis Solemnibus aderat die 30 mensis Novembris.
Eodem etiam anno novum instituit Centrum pro Spiritualitate,
et partem ecclesiae Cathedralis ornandam curavit.

Spiritualitatem rem maximi momenti esse reputabat atque
nutrimentum vitae spiritualis populi dioeceseos. Assidue paro-
ecias et scholas visitando opera dabat, praedicando, alloquendo,
auscultando, fideles hortando. Sustinere sacerdotes suos officium suum primarium censebat; iuvenes in Ecclesia sua sustinere
responsabilitatem specialem et prioritatem habebat. Inde a primis
diebus electionis suae sollicitus erat de rebus educationis et domi
et per totam nationem. Saepe de educatione catholica scripsit
et locutus est, cum agnosceret partem vitalem educationis in
missione Ecclesiae universa et in societate.

Actionem dioecesanam instituit quae coordinaret promov-
eretque responsa localia exigentiis socialibus; expandente morbo
A.I.D.S. dicto coetum creavit ubi illo morbo afflicti alii aliis auxilio
essent.

Londinii problema domo egentium levare nitebatur, creando
Centrum Transitus Diurni atque Centrum Cardinalis Hume pro
iuvenibus periclitantibus; Societatem Sancti Vincentii de Paul
hortatus est instituere illud de Paul Trust quod laboraret cum
iuvenibus sine domo in viis habitantibus. Praeses Conferentiae
Episcoporum dedit Ecclesiae Catholicae in Anglia et Cambria
periodum stabilitatis notabilis. Primo in Anglia et Cambria Congressui Pastorali Nationali praefuit, Processui quoque Inter Ecce-
lesias qui adiumentum erat in assequenda communi mente, communi corde, communi etiam voluntate, unitati Christianorum
faventibus. Suam Sanctitatem Papam Ioannem Paulum II invi-
tavit ut visitationem pastoralem faceret in Angliam et Cambriam
anno 1982. Post decisionem Ecclesiae Anglicanae mulieres ad
sacerdotium ordinandi, anno 1992 ipse partem notabilem egit
respondendo receptioni in Ecclesia Catholica et ordinationi cleri

the same year for the first time since the Reformation welcomed, to a Catholic celebration, an English Sovereign, Her Majesty Queen Elizabeth II, for Solemn Vespers on 30 November. In the same year he established a new Centre for Spirituality and embellished part of the Cathedral itself.

The Cardinal attached the highest importance to spirituality and the nourishment of the spiritual life of the people of the diocese. He devoted himself to visiting parishes and schools, to preaching and speaking, and to listening to and encouraging the faithful. He regarded the support of his priests as his primary duty and the support of young people in his Church as a particular responsibility and priority.

From the earliest days of his appointment, the Cardinal took a deep interest in educational matters, both domestically and nationally. He regularly wrote and spoke about Catholic education and recognised its vital role in the overall mission of the Church and to society.

He established a diocesan agency to co-ordinate and develop local responses to social needs, and in response to the spread of AIDS, the Cardinal established a self help group for people with AIDS.

He strove to alleviate the problem of homelessness in London by the establishment of the Passage Day Centre and the Cardinal Hume Centre for young people at risk and encouraged the Society of St Vincent De Paul to establish the De Paul Trust to work with street homeless young people.

As President of the Bishops' Conference he gave the Catholic Church in England and Wales a period of remarkable stability. He presided over the first National Pastoral Congress in England and Wales and The Inter-Church Process which helped achieve a common mind, a common heart and a common will towards Christian unity. He invited His Holiness, Pope John Paul II, to undertake a pastoral visit to England and Wales in 1982. He played a significant part in responding to the reception in the Catholic Church and the ordination of married and unmarried former

prius Anglicani vel matrimonio coniuncti vel non. Duobus documentis doctrinalibus magni momenti producendis praesidebat, videliecet Bonum Commune, de doctrina Sociali Ecclesiae Catholicae, et Unus Panis, Unum Corpus, de Eucharistia instructio, edita coniuncte cum Conferentiis Scotiae et Hiberniae. Ut Praeses Consilii Conferentiae Episcoporum Europae, intimo modo laborabat cum futuro Patriarcha Orthodoxo Alexei, et Russiam multoties visitavit. Cum communitate Iudaica vincula fortia et intima confecit et relationes bonas sustinebat. Anno 1986 aderat congressui extraordinario ducum religiosorum mundi, in civitate Assisi convocato a Papa Ioanne Paulo II. Ultimis vitae annis magis magisque certus fiebat de necessitate inter varias fides dialogi quem paris momenti censebat cum relationibus ecumenicis. Anno 1997 favebat formationi illius Operis, Trium Fidium Forum, congregantis Mussulmanos, Christianos et Iudaeos.

In corrigendis erroribus iustitiae legalis Cardinalis propugnator evenit; operam dabat ut condemnatio certe aboleretur illorum quattuor virorum vulgo "The Guildford Four". Profunde anxius erat de effectibus debiti aerarii internationalis, de difficultatibus Hiberniae Septentrionalis, de commercio armorum et de praeservandis iuribus humanis. Fortiter etiam favebat laboribus peractis pro iustitia inter gentes, prohibitioni usus in confessionalibus machinarum occultarum ab extra auscultandi causa, provisioni pro quaerentibus libertatem et expulsis a patria, iuri ad vitam infantium in utero et senium, magno momento matrimonii et familiae tamquam fundamentorum societatis, et curae personarum homosexualitate affectarum.

Auctor fuit multorum librorum, aliaque scripta breviora publicavit; a Mediis Communicationis multo existimatus est propter eius integritatem, spiritualitatem et conspicuam praestantiam religiosam.

Multis gradibus academicis honoratus erat Cardinalis: die 3 mensis Iunii anno 1999 a Sua Maiestate Regina Elizabeth II recepit Ordinem Meriti.

Anglican clergy after the decision of the Church of England to ordain women in 1992. He presided over two significant Conference teaching documents *The Common Good*, on social teaching in the Catholic Church, and *One Bread One Body*, a statement on the Eucharist issued jointly with the Scottish and Irish Bishops' Conferences. As President of the European Council of Episcopal Conferences he worked closely with the future Russian Orthodox Patriarch Alexei and visited Russia many times. He also established close links and maintained good relationships with the Jewish community. In 1986 the Cardinal attended the extraordinary meeting of world religious leaders called by Pope John Paul II in Assisi. In his later years he became increasingly convinced of the need to develop better inter-faith dialogue, which he put on a par with ecumenical relationships. He encouraged the formation of the *Three Faiths Forum* in 1997, bringing Muslims, Christians and Jews together.

The Cardinal became a champion for miscarriages of justice and sought to secure the quashing of the convictions of the Guilford Four. He was deeply concerned with the effect of international debt, the problems of Northern Ireland, the arms trade, and the preservation of human rights. He also strongly supported the work for racial justice, the prevention of the use of bugging devices in the confessional, the provision for asylum seekers and refugees, the right to life of the unborn and the aged, the importance of marriage and the family life as foundations of society, and care for homosexually oriented people.

He was the author of many books and articles and was greatly respected by the Media for his integrity, spirituality and outstanding religious leadership.

The Cardinal was awarded many honorary Degrees and, on 3 June 1999, he received the Order of Merit from Her Majesty, Queen Elizabeth II.

Cardinalis amor ludorum, per totam vitam perdurans, bene notus fuit.

Die 2 mensis Martii anno 1998, anno suo 75° completo, Cardinalis officii abdicationem obtulit: Papa Ioannes Paulus II ab eo quaesivit ut ultro aliquot annos in loco maneret.

Die 16 mensis Aprilis anno 1999 sacerdotibus suis scripsit nuntians se lethali tumore afflictum esse. Illos hortatus est his verbis, "Evangelium in nostra societate iterum vivere debet. Utinam gratia ista in Anno Sancto omnibus nobis concedatur. Vos, Patres Carissimi, in hac re assequenda primariam partem agendam habetis". Postquam Sacramenta receperat a suo Secretario Privato, Patre Jacobo Curry, vespere diei 17 mensis Iunii anno 1999 obdormivit in Domino.

Requiescat In Pace.

The Cardinal's life-long love of sport was well-known.

The Cardinal offered his resignation on 2 March 1998, on the completion of his seventy-fifth year. Pope John Paul II asked him to stay in place for several more years.

On 16 April 1999 he wrote to his priests and announced that he had terminal cancer. He admonished, 'The Gospel must live again in our society. May that grace be given to us all in the Holy Year. You, dear Fathers, have a key role to play in that.'

After receiving the Sacraments from his Private Secretary, Father James Curry, on the evening of 17 June 1999, he fell asleep in the Lord.

May he rest in peace.

Select Bibliography

Works by Basil Hume

Basil in Blunderland. 1997. Reprint, Brewster, MA: Paraclete Press, 1999.

Cardinal Basil Hume: In My Own Words. Edited by T. de Bertodano. London: Hodder & Stoughton, 1999.

Cardinal Hume: A Spiritual Companion. Compiled by L. Kelly. Reprint, Brewster, MA: Paraclete Press, 2001.

Footprints of the Northern Saints. London: Darton, Longman and Todd Ltd, 1996.

Hope from the Cross: Reflections on Jesus' Seven Last Words. Edited by L. Kelly. Reprint, Ijamsville, MD: Word Among Us Press, 2010.

In Praise of Benedict 480–1980 A.D. 1981. Reprint, Leominster: Ampleforth Abbey Press/Gracewing, 1996.

The Intentional Life. Brewster, MA: Paraclete Press, 2003.

Light in the Lord: Reflections on the Priesthood. 1991. Reprint, Collegeville: Liturgical Press, 1993.

The Mystery of Love. 1996. Reprint, Brewster, MA: Paraclete Press, 2001.

The Mystery of the Cross. 1998. Reprint, Brewster, MA: Paraclete Press, 2000.

The Mystery of the Incarnation. Reprint, Brewster, MA: Paraclete Press, 2000.

Remaking Europe: The Gospel in a Divided Continent. London: Society for Promoting Christian Knowledge, 1994.

Searching for God. 1978. Reprint, Leominster: Ampleforth Abbey Press/Gracewing, 2002.

To Be a Pilgrim: A Spiritual Notebook. 1984. Reprint, London: Society for Promoting Christian Knowledge, 2009.

Towards a Civilization of Love: Being the Church in Today's World. 2nd ed. London: Hodder and Stoughton, 1995.

A Turning to God. Edited by P. Hardcastle Kelly. Collegeville: Liturgical Press, 2007.

Works on Basil Hume

Butler, C., ed., *Basil Hume: By His Friends*. London: Fount, 1999.

Castle, T., *Basil Hume: A Portrait*. London: HarperCollins, 1987.

Charles, W., *Basil Hume: Ten Years On*. London: Burns & Oates, 2009.

Howard, A., *Basil Hume: The Monk Cardinal*. London: Headline, 2005.

Mortimer, J., 'Birthday Greetings from a Monk', in *In Character: Interviews with Some of the Most Influential and Remarkable Men and Women of our Time*. New York: Penguin Books, 1984, pp. 87–93.

Nichols, K., *Pilgrimage of Grace: Cardinal Basil Hume 1923–1999*. Dublin: Veritas Publications, 2000.

Noel, G., *Cardinal Basil Hume*. London: Hamish Hamilton, 1984.

Stanford, P., *Cardinal Hume and the Changing Face of English Catholicism*. 1993. Reprint, London: Geoffrey Chapman, 1999.

Walsh, M., 'George Basil Hume', in *The Westminster Cardinals: The Past and the Future*. London: Burns & Oates, 2008, pp. 195–222.

1   Father, forgive them for they know not what they do

    He forgave because he loved
    Love is the whole explanation
    of all he did.
    Love it was that made him live
    like us
    And experience
    Suffering and death
    All things human ~~too~~
    have different meaning now
    Suffering - ~~not~~ to purify
    Death the gateway to life.
    Because Thou had didst suffer
    and die
    For us.
    How little we understand,
    How insensitive
    Ungrateful
    Forgive us, we know not what we do

2

Amen I say to you,
This day you will be with me in paradise

For the thief,
So much suffering,
~~such~~ brutal punishment,
The gnawing anxiety of a mis-spent life;
nothing now but darkness and death;
Then the simple reassuring words.
Bewildered first
Un believing
He slowly ~~finds~~ ~~the~~ light and life;
No terror now in pain,
his heart is at peace,
his mind at rest
And his dying lips
~~bless the author of life~~.
bless his new-found Master
The author of life.

Woman behold thy son , ~~son~~ Then behold thy mother

3

His hour had come
And hers too ;
She had given him life ;
Now she ~~stands~~ and ~~watches~~,
As life slowly and painfully
~~left~~ leaves him .
The sight of it
~~pierces~~ like a sword
Her mother's heart .
This ~~is~~ her hour of agony,
One with his .
make One ~~Her suffering~~ pains ~~is mother~~ her again,
of ~~All~~ sinful humans
~~are~~ born to newness of life
in the death of her ~~only~~ son.

4.   My God, My God why hast Thou forsaken me?

He has been stripped of all,
but who minds being stripped
if God be still possessed?
This is the most frightening moment.
For he suffers now
the desolation
of abandonment,
the hideous emptiness
of life without God.
A great mystery.
We cannot understand.
A great consolation, though,
For those ~~who~~ called to share this trial —
in the depths of human sadness
and great darkness of soul,
When death is more welcome
than life,
Self no longer counts —
The soul finds God,
    rather
    is found by him —
    and lives

170

5 | I thirst

He longed for
parched lips to be moistened
his aching thirst to be slaked;
Less a pain that
than the sorrow of love ignored,
Kindness spurned.
He had longed
To give much —
No bitterness ~~for him~~
only ~~too~~ sadness
~~loneliness is no desert~~
He has drunk the chalice of sorrow.
They quench how
With vinegar and gall.

6   It is finished

He has completed the work
given him by the Father;
Soon he will be glorified
with that glory
Which was his
before the world began -
The Son of God
True God and True man.
Man's debt to God is paid;
The wrongs wrought by Sin ~~are~~
are now put right;
Human nature in him
passes through death to life,
and itself will share
the glory of God -
inherit the kingdom,
~~&~~ His work is done -
~~and~~ leaves his followers
to tread like him
the way to Calvary;
Sustained by him
and guided,
each one makes his way to ~~God~~ God.

7   Father, into thy hands I commend my spirit

        The last moment has come
        They can hurt him no more
        He has passed already
        Beyond the pains of this world
        Serene
        Peaceful
        Full of joy
        He gives himself
        in his last breath
        Back to the hands that first
        fashioned the earth's dust into man
        They will take him down
        and bury him,
          But the tomb of death
          will not hold captive
          the giver of life.
          Not for him the return to dust,
          but the triumph of
          Resurrection.